Garden Art

Garden Art

THE PERSONAL PURSUIT OF ARTISTIC REFINEMENTS, INVENTIVE CONCEPTS, OLD FOLLIES AND NEW CONCEITS FOR THE HOME GARDENER

Lorraine Marshall Burgess

BLACK-AND-WHITE PHOTOGRAPHS AND PENLINE SKETCHES
BY THE AUTHOR
COLOR PHOTOGRAPHS BY GUY BURGESS

WALKER AND COMPANY

New York

*To my father, James Benjamin Marshall,
who, by quiet example,
has shown me the joys of gardening*

Library of Congress Cataloging in Publication Data

Burgess, Lorraine Marshall.
  Garden art.

  Bibliography: p. 187
  Includes index.
  1. Gardens—Design. 2. Garden structures.
  3. Garden ornaments and furniture. I. Title.
  SB473.B739 1981   712′.6   80-51992
  ISBN-0-8027-0665-7

First published in the United States of America
in 1981 by the Walker Publishing Company, Inc.

Published simultaneously in Canada by Beaverbooks,
Limited, Don Mills, Ontario.

ISBN: 0-8027-0665-7

Library of Congress Catalog Card Number: 80-51992

Designed by Joyce Cameron Weston

Printed in the United States of America

10 9 8 7 6 5 4 3 2 1

Contents

Introduction

The garden you create may be the most personal thing you do in your life, so relish the experience. Ease away from the dos and don'ts of gardening and follow your natural inclinations. Work alone if you prefer or consult on projects with your family. If your ideas are scoffed, wait patiently until the world catches up with them. Coast along in the midst of your fantasies for the best results. Even if the end product only approximates your intent, you should find satisfaction in 'almost'.

The art of self-expression is coming into its own in the gardens and backyards of America. Whether this is because of travel restrictions or outside pressures, it is difficult to say, but many gardeners are discovering previously-hidden talents and they are bringing them to flower along with their annuals and perennials. To their own surprise they are shaping new summer houses and fashioning unexpected refinements. They are creating ornaments and embellishments simply for their own pleasure and amusement.

Garden art, they are learning, is their rightful heritage, a practice that has been followed for centuries by garden-makers escaping from the worries of their own times.

The dangers inherent in this book may be greater than is at first apparent. My aim is to involve you in the creative aspects of garden art. I have no conscience, I am presuming that you and your kin will benefit from the entrapment. If I seem to press too hard, you certainly have the privilege of backing away. I admit to being smitten with all forms of garden art and I may work in insidious ways to persuade you to the same commitment.

Don't claim you haven't the talent. Our brand of art needs many kinds of skills, from primitive wood-carving to expert cabinetry. It flourishes because of the miscellaneous knowledge of horticulturists, garden historians and archeologists studying human behavior and culture. It is sparked by persons with quaint and playful ideas, and by inventive artists having amateur or professional status. Garden art needs artisans and craftsmen who can translate pen-line designs into actual structures or adornments. And beyond this, garden art greets with enthusiasm all who dwell upon dreams and fantasies.

If we are labeled esoterics, we can't take offense. We are what the word implies— members of an inner group, a charmed circle of disciples or scholars. It is true that we are inward-facing and our circle is charmed. But it is a wide one, open to all who care to join. If you wish to escape, count this as your last warning; if you want to join in, consider this your first invitation.

LMB

CHAPTER ONE

Creations

Art is a talent that lies dormant in many of us and deserves probing. Don't let your skills be suppressed by the chores of weeding and mowing; exercise them and find the pleasures and amusements this exercise can provide.

If you question your abilities, at least try them out in the seclusion of your garden place. Experiment at your leisure, away from the critical eye and the unkind word. Work slowly if you prefer, or plunge into a project and work feverishly if it seems beneficial. Few will be aware of your preoccupation.

Start by doing something creative, something you would classify as untypical behavior . . . Sand down the rough edges on a new bench and repaint it in a muted color. Carve a small bird on the top of a stake to use as an ornamental hose guard at the corner of your perennial garden.

If you are the type that demands immediate results, turn to something horticultural. Get out your spade and move a special clump of blooming golden iris across the garden to be replanted in a slot of sunlight that prevails there in the late afternoon. Do the transplant quickly, press in place and water well. With this and normal care, the golden blooms should continue to flower in their new limelight without missing a beat, and the plant should survive without mishap.

Make It Spectacular

No matter what project you choose for your first creative venture, make it spectacular enough to send you on your way. If you keep these new excursions secret, you will no doubt deny yourself the advice of well-meaning friends but you may also avoid a lot of misleading criticism. Form, instead, your own strong opinions. Probe your natural inclinations. Unearth any desires,

suppressed or otherwise, and nurture any whims or idle follies that come to the surface.

If you need still another reason, realize that artistic exercises can be therapy. Creativity can become so absorbing that it serves as an escape mechanism, shielding you meanwhile from the ills of our disturbing society. Without driving a single mile you can escape to an idyllic land of high aspirations and modest accomplishments. Here you can tend your plants, your pots or your paintings in peaceful isolation.

Once you feel at ease with your new endeavors, you may want to study the practices of other artists. Some choose their design subjects by lot. They work without reason and allow their subconscious to surface in undisciplined color, strange shapes or an extraordinary line. Working as in a dream, they create images which they later claim intellectually. They do their thing, they feel free, they are free.

Your own approach to such exercises can be gradual, if it is in your nature, or abrupt if you fancy quick discovery. You know your own drives and the extent of your current skills. Keep reaching for new revelations or sit and ponder those already acquired.

Creativity is sometimes described as the avoidance of the probable and the skirting of the predictable. This can be a good beginning, if it sounds right to you. We must each worry along in our own way. Some wag claimed that gardening is a matter of 'trowel and error', the doing and undoing of mistakes. The same might be said for garden art.

Reach for New Ideas

Even if you achieve your stride quickly, don't stop reaching. Read books, visit museums and galleries, and thumb art magazines for inspiration. Ponder the techniques and methods of those you encounter. Learn their doctrines. Architect Robert Venturi, for instance, prefers to work "with elements that are hybrid rather than pure, compromising rather than clean, and distorted rather than straightforward." One theory like that could set you off in a new direction for months.

St. Francis found inspiration by "hobnobbing with the trees and flowers, sitting on the land, observing and learning to draw." That may be the right approach for you.

There are hints to be found in peculiar places. Even advertisers offer unsolicited advice. One cigarette ad suggested that we "look for fresh promise in familiar things, and use individual imagination, creativity and originality."

Don't stay home and be a recluse. Communication with other artists can be beneficial. As with plants, there are advantages in cross-pollination. Talk with your counterparts, exchange ideas, pool your discoveries and compare your accomplishments. From these seeds your learning and your base of understanding will quickly flower.

If you favor the abstract, you might find guidance in the words of Robert Motherwell, the New York painter who considers the process of painting "an adventure, without preconceived ideas, on the part of persons of intelligence and passion." Others say it another way. They start with a fabrication and then aim to make it real.

Dare To Be Daring

No matter which tangent you follow, make a definite assertion. Veer away from the tame, the vague and the colorless. Take heart from the maxim that says "it is worse to be irresolute than to be wrong."

If, after all this coaxing, you are still hesitating, think of your children, if you have them. If they should come up short on imagination, the fault could be yours. This because you had not openly expressed, in their presence, your own fancies as they occurred to you.

If you find yourself inept and a slow learner, do the best you can and let the rest come. Gather reassurance where you can find it and take confidence in the words of Will Rogers, "Everybody is ignorant, only in different lines."

Because so much of garden art is visual or sensual, it is difficult to present verbally. It speaks its own language to some, to others it stands mute. The ideas offered herein in words, photos and sketches are intended to please you so much you will undertake similar excursions of your own. Enjoy, enjoy.

Make the best use of land

Every garden is in itself a work of art, a source of pride and opportunity for its maker. Its prime purpose is delight, a place rich in gifts and favors. No matter how far you travel it will wait for your return. It gives you a sense of security and develops within you an affection for all things alive and growing.

Don't complain if you have difficult land. Some of the best gardens are put together from uneven and irregular parts. Strive to accent these differences and take pleasure in the interplay of light on dark, soft on sharp, tender on tough and rounded on flat.

If rock-strewn land is what you have most of, create a pool in the spaces between and keep the water flowing with a gravity design and a small pump. Add a spouting fish, a few water plants and make a few places where you can stand to enjoy the sparkle, close up.

If you should fall heir to a piece of an apple orchard, be grateful. Make it the focus of your garden design. Find excuse for frequent celebrations as growth moves from bud to leaf, from flower to fruit and finally to golden autumn color. Seed the ground beneath with grasses, even raise a few sheep to graze the land and eat their keep, it's not as radical a project as it sounds. Then as a final gesture, plant islands of strawberries near a crossway point where friends can congregate and enjoy your bounty.

Naturalize a meadow garden if you have open, sunny land. Plant native flower seeds or plantlets at three-week intervals so they can mature and bloom continuously over several summer months. Allow the flowers to bloom and go to

seed before mowing the land, or better still, let the grasses grow tall so your children can make trails to play in.

For a standard lot, dream up a pleasant framing and a vista. Make fencing or shrub enclosure an early consideration. Arrange your plantings carefully so they do not intrude on any desirable views. If no good views exist, create your own points of focus within your boundaries. If you are blessed with a south-facing slope, enjoy the advantages of a warm and extended season. If your land slopes toward the north, plan early how you can cope with harsh winds and shaded ground.

Your Garden Is for You

Before you start to grade and smooth your lot to conform to neighboring properties, consider retaining the natural ups and downs that give dis-

tinction to your land. Then face your garden inward for your own pleasure rather than toward the street to please the passerby. The day you think of your plot as a garden instead of a front or back yard, you have become a gardener.

If you dislike fences and want privacy, shape an earth mound around your lot and plant the *berm* with sound-absorbing succulents to lessen traffic noise. Trim existing trees upward and make a haven for yourself within the ring.

Keep in mind always that your garden is and should be a natural adjunct to your house. Use it to extend your living spaces and your social life. Even at Versailles the palace was too small for royal parties without the use of the gardens.

If you are obliged to turn inward for garden focus, consider developing a traditional garden of Japanese, Colonial, or European origin. Strive for authenticity, as is evident in this Enshu lantern and water basin setting. The stepping stones are considered essential for standing upon when putting in the light, the tree with the extended branch for partially concealing the scene.

Interrupt the View

Your garden should never appear so open that it seems needless to go into it. There need to be shrubs and trees that interrupt the view, so as to tempt your visitors further. Designing a garden can be an accepted responsibility or a heady experience. The second approach is much preferred. Be inventive or experimental; just remember that what you do at the beginning will affect the success of all that follows. If you feel unsure, consult with other skilled local gardeners or a professional landscape designer. They can offer guidance that you can follow yourself, or contract to do the work for you.

Study the Site

Become thoroughly acquainted with your site. Learn the merits of the soil, natural drainage routes and the paths of the sun, winter and summer. If you have too much shade, modify any untoward aspirations. Be creative, but within the discovered restrictions. Relate the garden design proportions in some way to those of the house. While the man with a small house and a large garden is doubly blessed, related scale makes for future harmonies.

If your land is cut by a drainage ditch, reshape it a bit so it meanders in a natural way and then plant it with jonquils, marsh marigolds and violets for a spring surprise. As energy allows, add wildflowers to grace other seasons.

If the entire project seems too big, start around your rear terrace with precise design and then ease into less formal shapes at mid-garden and further vagueness toward the back boundary. This leaves you with the option of adding more specific form later or letting the whole design become looser if you discover that is more in keeping with your true spirit.

To succeed in your creative ventures, share your dreams with your family and solicit their assistance. Compromise may be essential if there is a demand for a basketball backstop, a drying yard or a tree house.

If this is a retirement project, consider the theory of planting large or fast-growing trees to clothe a raw lot quickly. Interplant this with

slower-growing varieties of long-term value. The weed trees are cut down as the better trees mature. By then you may be needing your own firewood to keep warm.

Plan also to enjoy your garden in the winter. Strive to make at least one window view as attractive as possible, but don't be content with this. Put on your boots and go tramping in the snow, being careful to stay on paths so as not to crush enterprising plant shoots. With a camera in hand study stems and seedheads in their hoarfrost dress. Get a stepladder and sculpt a tall bear. Pour cold water over your work of art so it will freeze deeper, then sculpt if further on subsequent afternoons. Your neighbors may love your bear, and forgive you for your selfish garden.

Use the site well

After you have your grand plan down on graph paper to exact proportions, take it out into your garden and chart out the spaces with stakes and a chalk line, or use bricks or large stones to mark the corners. Then live with these markings for a week or more while you ponder the width of the flowerbeds, the convenience of the paths, and the size of the terrace. This is important because plans tend to seem different in real life than they are on paper. Be forewarned. Review your proposed plantings, sticking a cane or an umbrella in the ground where an ornamental tree is to go. Study all lines of sight to determine whether the tree, as it matures, will hide the utility pole you hate or interrupt a view you wish to keep. Modify the design as necessary, or change it drastically if need be. While these changes may seem disruptive, they are not so grave as they would be after the beds are installed in a wrong place, or the trees have grown.

If yours is an arid climate, guard against water shortages early. Shape your lawn to a shallow saucer so it will catch and hold all the precious water it receives. Locate your house downspouts beside major trees so they will receive more than their fair share of rainfall. Now that rain gutters are formed up on the site, this is not a difficult thing for a builder to do. Discover your most favorable microclimates: out of the hot sun, away from harsh winds or where the water drainage naturally converges to support greener plant materials. Use them as family gathering places.

All of us have an instinct for enclosed spaces, walled havens for the protection of our kin. I like to think that in earlier reincarnations we lived behind castle walls. Whatever the impulse, it still prevails. We need sanctuaries to serve as buffers against irritations we cannot control. We also seek to maintain contact with nature. This is not easy to do, but gardening seems to be the answer for many.

People Are Part of a Garden

As you make your plans, do not overlook your own presence and that of your family and friends in your garden. Landscape designers define gardening as the process of arranging people on the land. It's a matter of color and movement. Perhaps that is why we all look so decorative when we are playing croquet, pitching horse-shoes, or drinking tea in the garden.

Don't fight the people problem. Strive to create places where humans would naturally want to be. If your friends, with drinks in hand, tend to gather under a particular tree, don't try to lead them to the new deck you have built in the outer precincts. Instead, before your guests come again, build in greater comfort in the place where they were first inclined to congregate. They may get around to seeing your distant deck on another day.

Use anticipation as a device to move people about. This is a valid theory in garden design. It tempts us to move from one garden space to another, always in search of something more. But for this theory to succeed, each section of the garden must offer both a reason for lingering and a temptation to move on. It becomes a subtle game of tug of war. You must also plan some kind of grand finale. It isn't fair to offer nothing to look at after you have tempted people to the far end. Remember, we all love a mystery, a curving path that disappears, a brief glimpse of a flowered space, an overlook at the rim of a hill or a place to sit near the edge of a pond.

When views are limited and the land is bleak, create enticements within the garden's own width and breath. Shape your beds to flow with the natural contours of the site and direct attention toward your favorite garden planting. Any feature that tempts you to roam the area is considered a valid garden device. Measure the success of your own design by determining the route you prefer and then see how many of your visitors follow that path, unassisted.

Borrowed Views Are Bonuses

Make free use of borrowed views. An interruption of your fence line can reveal your neighbor's bold stand of forsythia as it blooms each spring in all its golden splendor. Clear your line of sight toward the sugar maples down the block, so you can enjoy them as an autumn dividend. Such surreptitious borrowing has further benefits. When your neighbors discover what you are doing they will most likely be flattered by the attention, and praise you for your discernment. Borrowing, incidentally, is one of the few examples of no-maintenance gardening. There is no weeding, no fertilizing and no watering. However, you may want to volunteer to help with the pruning if the scene begins to look ragged.

The other spaces we work with are fluid. With

trees and shrubs we have the means to interrupt them at will. Knowing this, we should be careful to avoid excessive staccato rhythms that accelerate the tempo of our lives.

Instead, be a lazy magician. Create a quiet, flowery place where you can relax unobserved and still oversee the children in their play area. Develop a space warm enough for afternoon napping and another cool enough to provide escape from summer heat waves. Trim big trees artfully to bring light into your space. Architect I.M. Pei, in speaking of light, said, "There are always surprises. When you work with God, you can't go wrong."

If you are dealing with a treeless site, build a pergola strong enough to support an old-fashioned two-way swing like this one in Iowa's Amana Colony, and a burgeoning grape vine heavy with fruit. The vine provides thick shade in summer and admits warm sunlight in winter, should you want to sit in the garden then.

Each shaft of light we unleash seems a personal victory. With so few constraints in a garden, we tend to unearth mysteries within ourselves. As soon as we begin to think of ourselves as almighty we discover that there are other differences brought on by the shift of light and the change of seasons. No condition is ever quite the same, and we have little to do with the changing.

Earth Berms as 'Fences'

If you are starting with a new house on a raw site, an earth berm may be better than a fence and cost little or nothing. While the builders are excavating for your house, arrange to have the surplus dirt distributed around the roadside corners of your property. Shape and rake it into natural looking mounds and plant it with sturdy ground covers, particularly on the outer slopes. If there are rocks in the transported soil, attempt to use them as placed. Just be sure they are anchored in place. In your newly-created inward space, plant the slopes with colorful flowers and a few trees as further strategic screening. If you have heavy traffic problems, the earth mounds will also deaden the sounds or deflect them into the air above, away from your ears. Plot the drainage of berms carefully so you do not end up with a dam site and an unplanned lake.

Through the centuries artistic drive has expressed itself in strange and delightful ways. Earlier gardeners have built waterways and fountains, grottos and labyrinths, all without benefit of heavy earth-moving equipment. They have shaped tree-lined tunnels as allées, planted trees to make a forest bosket, and patterned flower beds as parterres. They have indulged in topiary pruning and in training orchard trees into fan, rope and grid designs.

Good beginnings

Now that you have picked up momentum, don't start taking the everyday excitements of gardening for granted. You must continue to develop your talents. Find the ideal way to exploit your garden situation. Promote the idea of an intimate place, fenced for privacy, and just right for sunning or tubbing. Arrange and rearrange facilities for your greatest pleasure. Don't ever feel committed to a fixed plan.

Choose plants that you find particularly appealing even if they do not relate well with each other. Select flowers in hues that make you feel good. If gardening has been one long, dull chore for you, take drastic measures. Get out of the rut.

Intensify the good qualities the land possesses. If you have purchased a second-generation garden, attempt first to restore its latent image. Work plant by plant to recapture old magic, but allow yourself to inject a few conceits of your own, even if they are not exactly appropriate.

If it is in your nature to go backward in time, and your site allows, turn to the styles of our forefathers. Start with a favored Colonial design and adhere as closely as possible to paving and fencing patterns. Just remember that you do not have the slave labor needed to do the pruning and clipping many of these gardens require.

To garden the wooded hillside that has been thrust upon you by an accident of fate, cut a series of connecting terraces by digging into the slope and spilling the spoils over the outside rim. Back and fill, pack and tamp. Add serpentine paths and flights of stairs between your several plateaus. Then plant the entire slope with sun or shade plants suitable to the particular condition.

Fill the nooks and crannies around the terraces with impatiens, Hostas and fibrous begonias and see that they all get enough water.

On a level site, go Elizabethan. Lay out a knot garden of useful herbs and plant the interwoven rows with thyme, basil, oregano, chives and lavender. Then frame the patterned area with needled and broadleaf evergreens for continuing beauty through the winter.

A Plant Sanctuary

If you are a zealous environmentalist, suppress your frustrations by collecting all the native plants in your region in seed and seedling form as a means of propagating and preserving them for future generations. Within the limits of your garden space attempt to reproduce the growing conditions from which the individual plants were gathered. There are opportunities for innovative and legal gathering. Get permission to collect from Federal agencies holding regional land, and from highway and dam contractors about to unleash their earth-moving equipment on a nearby project.

If you have the patience, the time and the temperament to wait and watch for twenty years, plant out saplings of oak, hickory and sycamore to start a future forest. As the trees begin to mature, add shrubs and native ornamentals to create a typical understory and provide the protection needed to grow ferns, moss and local ground covers.

The Pleasures of Plants

Become acquainted early with the deep pleasures to be found in the plants themselves. Explore the similarities and differences in tree and leaf forms, in rough and smooth bark and in delicate and sturdy framework. Study the silhouettes and linear character of your favorite trees and become aware of the shifts that occur in their leaf color from one season to the next.

While these are all good beginnings they are but passive responses to Nature's natural habits and require very little contribution on your part. To assume a more active role in your garden space, reach out. Impose your taste, your color sense and your creative skills on every project you tackle.

Lay a careful path of selected stone, enlarge your terrace space by adding a border of brick or tile around the existing slab. Combine two kinds of flowering plants in a way you have never seen done before. Avoid the natural tendency to discount your own skills. Use your talents boldly.

Dare to be an artist in your own domain. Work quietly and inconspicuously but bring an intensity to your efforts. This can surely propel you along to find better solutions. Enjoy the excitement of bold rebellion and strange departures. You can be uninhibited, so long as you choose.

Aim to focus on a strong feature and simultaneously solve a problem. The garden in the photograph on page 16 demonstrates the advantages of this theory. The slope behind this hilltop house was too steep for terrace use and there were two fine old live oak trees, twenty feet out, that deserved protection. The solution was creative, although it now seems obvious. Half-circle tree wells were built around the uphill side of each oak, and built tall enough to serve as bench tops on the finished terrace. Then the area between the retaining walls and the house was packed with soil, gravel and sand to bring it up to terrace grade, and finished with brick pavers.

While the hired work was being done the owners searched out a fine collection of succulents for repotting in terra cotta bowls and flowerpots. These they placed around the curved benches as living ornaments. The trees were saved, the view preserved and the terrace enjoyed, all because of innovative design. Other views of this terrace are shown in Color Plates 15 and 27.

A similar retaining-wall solution was found for a garden with a spectacular canyon view. Two lichen stone walls were raised up along parallel contour lines and the area between brought up to terrace level with soil and pea-sized gravel. Chairs and a table were set out near the rim wall and overhanging trees reached out to shade the entire area. The curving upper wall includes a long bench and a gracious flight of steps, as shown in Color Plate 18. The stairs lead up to another terrace at the back of the house.

An urban dooryard garden in the Old Town section of Chicago, shown below, was enclosed with a high brick wall at the front sidewalk line. The gated entry is at one side of the garden and the front steps of the house at the other, preventing passersby from looking into the house. A pair of old elevator doors from a razed office building were hung as gates for the garden. Other wrought iron fencing finds a second use as window guards for the ground-level apartment.

Turn your energies toward physical exploration. Become acutely aware of your sense of touch, taste and smell. If this all sounds slightly sinful, be reassured. All I am advising is rebellion against anything that makes gardening seem a chore—dandelions, crab grass and mowing. To understand the intent of this rebellion, deliberately avoid any chores that take a lot of muscle and no brains.

Gardening may be the poor man's pleasure, but it is also the thinking man's art. A garden is such good, clean fun that no one, man or woman, should be denied its privileges.

Start with a strong feature

Distinguished gardens win this designation because of the unique features they possess. If the bones of the design are good, the garden will hold together, but its features must be strong and used with authority.

Perhaps the strongest and most typical feature in American gardens today is a broad terrace, patio or deck. This has been true for some time and, as money grows tighter and houses become smaller again, entertainment areas out-of-doors are providing economical space for more gracious living. With increasing fuel costs many gardeners are migrating in the south and the west. This makes their garden space doubly valuable. Builders are finding that most saleable design today makes it easy for the buyer to get out of the house and into the garden.

Of equal concern is designing a garden to meet one's own social patterns. If you prefer a quiet place where two or three friends might sit and talk together, your needs are simple. If you are instead the big-party type, you will need a broad

lawn for entertaining. This determined, you should choose raised flowerbeds as a prime feature. Build brick walls, bench high, around each bed for good looks and plant protection from dancing or stumbling feet. Flowers will be on display closer to eye level and the bench-high shelf will give your guests places to sit down and smell the flowers.

A Welcome to Friends

If you have very little space to garden but still like to entertain, convert your front yard into a vestibule—a dooryard garden. Add extra paving blocks on either side of your walkway, some flowering plants and fragrant herbs, and a pair of benches in a small alcove. Enclose the space with a solid or a picket fence and think of the garden as a new room in your house. Then, when guests are expected, water down the area to freshen the flowers and exaggerate the scent of the herbs. This custom of watering the entry area is oriental, and is intended to make the guests feel welcome.

If your plot is flat and square, rely on strong design and good plant material to achieve distinction. The square kitchen garden at Colonial Williamsburg is divided into four equal parts and is dominated by a holly tree trimmed to a drum and dome shape. The central circle and its brick walkway is bordered by four different kinds of fruit trees, each bent and curved to a cordoned design. The geometric pattern is reinforced by brick paths that connect the several parts.

The espaliered pear tree is shown in close-up. (The others are apple, peach, and apricot.) The "ropes" grow from opposite branches on a single trunk and are held about eighteen inches off the ground with stakes. As well as being decorative, the fruit trees serve as barriers and protection for the vegetable rows in the four corners. Also at harvest time the fruit is easy to pick. Clumps of chives edge the brick walk, providing lavender tufts of bloom in May and June and tasty cuttings in almost any season.

The Challenge Is There

Cataloging artistic expression is difficult. There simply are too many ways to go. Because there are no rules, there are few inhibitions. The field of endeavor is wide open and waiting for you.

If the thought of being 'arty' makes you feel uncomfortable, call it something else. Think of it instead as a way of unboggling the mind, expressing

a gut notion, or going on a trip that makes you feel proud and alive on your home grounds.

I realize that anyone who tends a garden is creative already. All I hope to do is push you a little further. You are a likely candidate for the art world. As a gardener you are naturally sensitive, as a horticulturist you are strong on visualization and you must be inventive. I cannot guess where your aspirations have led you so far. You may be satisfying a need for peace and quiet, or you may be building a haven that will nourish your mind, comfort your body and delight your senses. Where your focus has been really doesn't matter. In becoming an artist, any of these pursuits add to your qualifications.

The sun, the soil and the plants are our first involvement. These growth attractions never fade. But as gardeners we always seem to want more, more excitements, more challenges and, hopefully, more delight. For me garden art is a pleasureful supplement.

You Set Your Limits

The desire to express one's self seems basic to gardeners, but don't allow yourself to be carried away. Concentrate on gestures that are unobtrusive and pleasant, never insistent. Gardens have

been described as controlled environments, but keep in mind that you are the control and these are your environs. Concentrate on small refinements, sensitive embellishments and inventive solutions. Projects will vary with each individual but they will give evidence of natural talents thoughtfully expressed within one's individual havens.

Water, used as a feature, is a special joy. This light-reflecting element will assume any form we prescribe. It is beautiful as a sparkling current or a slender stream. Meandering through a garden it becomes a unifying thread or a quiet mirror reflecting colors. Its use cannot be overrated, yet it is incorporated in too few designs. Many shy away in fear of engineering problems or because it takes more care and maintenance than they can afford.

This handsome bridge brings distinction to a pond in the Japanese Garden of the Missouri Botanical Garden in St. Louis. More and more gardeners are discovering that the studied proportions and thoughtful detailing used in the Far East is almost positive assurance of excellence. The zigzag design, *yatsuhashi,* is named for the eight bridges that spanned a tenth century river with eight channels. The plank bridges crossed marshy ground where iris grew.

An oriental design, no matter how pristine, will appear strange if it is set down, cheek by jowl, with American gardens. It needs to be given a larger space or be isolated from neighbors with neutral plantings and special fencing.

Look for solutions

Soon many of us will need to design our gardens with the discipline of limits instead of the habit of plenty. There will be energy shortages, water shortages and fewer chemicals for fertilization. We will need to grow trees and shrubs as much for the oxygen they provide as for their beauty. Since plants make our air breathable, our survival may in time depend upon our gardening instincts.

Every Garden Is Unique

If you are a scholar as well as an expectant gardener, you might study the eccentricities of your garden's climate through an entire year. Discover where the snow melts fastest, where the winds are sharpest and where water gathers naturally. Gauge the intensity of the summer sun and determine how much shading is needed. By gathering this knowledge in advance, you can build a better house and a finer garden.

Some of us are most creative when we're faced with problems. The Arizona artist who designed this concrete casting was looking for a material that would withstand hot sun and be impervious to strong winds. He wanted a fence strong and opaque enough to shelter his garden space. He chose to make a series of concrete panels, two inches thick and imprinted while wet with decorative patterns having a Mayan flavor. Before flowing the concrete, he scattered a layer of white quartz chips in a plywood form to decorate the back side, then added reinforcing wires to strengthen the casting and serve later as ties. When the panels were set and dry he stood them along a zigzag line with alternate facings, and then tied the reinforcing wires together at each joint.

Early Arrivals Could Choose

As you travel around the country you may notice that early settlers appear to have chosen fine garden sites. But this was in part accidental. They looked for the spring or the stream that flourished there, the south slope for its solar warmth and its protection from harsh winds. They needed the wood lot for timber and fuel and the rock all around for building foundations. If we had to make a choice today for the same reasons, we would probably select a similar site.

But these homesteading choices are no longer

available. The best we seem able to do is cultivate a wilding garden—this as a kind of gesture to the cult of the wilderness. It also makes us realize what a small role we play on the planet Earth.

Answers for the Finding

No matter what the problems in gardening, there are usually good solutions. Land can be too rocky, too dry or too windblown. If it is too wet there are at least two or three alternatives. You can drain it with a tile field or fill it to a higher level. You can make it into a bog garden by digging shallow ponds or narrow channels to drain the higher ground. Then plant it with lilies and other water plants and build routes for walking on the hummocky land.

If you live in a town like New Orleans where the water table is close to ground level, design a garden with raised beds. Put together a series of frames with two-by-twelve-foot boards and set them on level ground in a pattern of your own choosing. Fill each 'box' with good garden loam and plant flowers that like plenty of moisture.

This accomplished, add a 3-inch layer of crushed rock to the paths between the boxes and you are well on your way to having a garden.

You can even create a garden under a flight of stairs. Accept the challenge. Bring in a load of garden soil and plant the area with shade plants, ferns, camillias, and begonias—whatever grow well in your region.

Sometimes a problem provides its own solution. Here a south-facing porch was flooded with too much sunlight in the wintertime. It became necessary to add a grid panel to the roof line to counter the sun's rays. As soon as the grid was attached the owner realized that it would make a fine place to grow grapes. The vines soon climbed upward to form a dense mass of foliage and beautiful translucent green light during the summer months. It was also a distinct sensual pleasure to reach up and pick a cluster of grapes as the crop ripened.

The charcoal cooker is an old riveter's forge. It can be fired up with a hand-crank and the added heat cooks chicken just right in the Dutch oven.

Creations with fine detailing

Garden decoration and detailing can enliven and brighten your life. Granted, such refinements may be considered a minor art, but they deserve more doing.

With each project completed we become more confident of our judgment and taste. We develop know-how and skills; craftsmanship becomes an important goal. Such exercises run second to our interest in growing plants, but the new standards we acquire can help us with horticultural detailing as well. In fact attention to detail is vital to all aspects of full-scale gardening.

Gardening is a continuum. We are never done with it nor would we choose to be. Each small triumph generates another effort. We discover other applications for a theory and extend our efforts from trees to shrubs to plants to paving. The days roll happily from one new spring to another.

The more you learn of detailing the more you want to know. As in all garden art, there is no saturation point.

Rewards of Labor

The laying and mortaring of thick flagstone is back-breaking work. It takes muscle and understanding. To make the steps easy to climb, the risers are low and the treads deep enough to permit a natural stride. But even after the heavy work is completed the gardener has taken time to install an edging of echeveria, a fleshy-leafed

plant that is admired for its soft, textural form more than its token flowers.

Sometimes humid climatic conditions help your work. Here the twenty-inch concrete tiles are edged with standard brick, but the scene is enriched by a soft, emerald green moss that fills all crevices. The dense growth of the creeping perennial and the flowering cineraria makes the ordinary paving materials look rich and beautiful.

This exquisite garden makes use of cuttings of cypress saplings to mark the division between a bed of red clover and an area of white pebbles. The large rocks have been arranged to discourage the development of a short cut path. The large, concrete paving panels are separated by redwood strips and the concrete was embellished with multi-colored pebbles pressed into the mix while it was still wet.

If you are looking for projects to do, try adding ceramic tiles to the front face of concrete steps, scallop shells as an intermediate detail on a brick-edged flower bed, or a rough-hewn stone path to the back garden.

Search for private satisfactions

Create special pleasures for yourself. Ruffle the feathers of a ceramic hen by filling her innards with a robust planting of hen-and-chick Sempervivum. Every effort you make need not be a production. It is worthwhile developing modest satisfactions for yourself and no other.

At Christmas, as a gesture of good will to your garden, shape a wreath of pine and holly around a bright red candle on the terrace dining table. The season may be busy, and the days cold. It is likely that no one will notice what you have done. But it doesn't matter. You will have enjoyed being in touch with your garden place.

Year-round Satisfactions

In the spring, as soon as the tulips have come up far enough to show their locations, buy several flats of bright-faced pansies and plant them in the dull spaces between. The tulips will always stay at least two steps ahead of their new neighbors but will appreciate the company and the extra watering and attention they have gained along the way. These grace the Sarah Duke Gardens in Durham, North Carolina.

My own private pleasure in late spring is the pursuit of four-leaf clovers. I closely guard several rug-sized beds of white clover in the middle

Friends and Neighbors

A widower of my acquaintance spent much of his time in his garden. He favored vines and grew them in profusion on fences and walls. He must have found peace there because he has small shrines hidden away among the vine leaves.

Another man, our neighbor, had a great love for nasturtiums, and he grew them well and free of black bugs. He would come to call on a summer evening with a fistful of flowers and stay only long enough to see that the pungent beauties were put in water. It was always a pleasant encounter.

A friend from California grew plain and fancy goldfish in a large pond with papyrus, arrowhead, water chestnut and umbrella palm. The fish were his special joy but their presence was not too evident unless he drew his guests to the water's edge and pointed them out. Their importance was a secret he shared with only a few.

of our lawn, and bemoan each mowing when the perfection of all clover leaves is damaged by the sharp blades. I have discovered that one patch is far 'luckier' than the others and I can find six or seven four-leafers in a minute or so. I bring my winnings into the house and place them in water in a porcelain eggcup where they last for days. When skeptical guests challenge their authenticity I take them out to the special patch and find them a quad-foil on the spot, with little effort.

A school teacher friend traveled during the summer, but she loved her spring garden. To magnify the importance of tiny blue squills or lavender crocus she planted them in the exotic company of semi-precious stones. What she could not find in the mountains she purchased at rock shops. First she arranged pink quartz, rose alabaster, and turquoise-colored amazonite in comfortable relationships and then tucked the tiny bulbs in the ground beside these warm monsters. She also planted slender pink tulips in the middle of a wide bed of sweet violets. Her front porch garden was a joy in the spring.

CHAPTER TWO

Plants

Of all the plants, trees are of course our first involvement. They people our gardens like actors in a play, playing major and minor roles. They contribute to our gardens in myriad ways. They stand as massive forms gently bending and swaying in the wind. In the early hours of morning their giant masses turn to gold as the sun rises. In the fading light of night their shadows comfort and enfold. Their shapes are endlessly different, from the vase-like forms of elm to the rounded oak, the oval hickory and the pyramids of pine, fir and spruce. Some frameworks are ragged, others symmetrical. Their size from seed to sapling is within the human scale but it changes to that of giants in maturity.

We love our gigantic companions for their strength and dignity or their fragile grace. We revel in their changing colors, their translucence and the many textures they possess. On occasion we grow alien stock or difficult ornaments as we are able, but we rely on trees native to our region to give our gardens the stability they would not have otherwise. We enjoy the wonder of robust growth and watch these trees in sunlight and shade as they reach to the sky.

Trees Are Basic

I urge you to study all that is offered and think of trees as your prime tools in creating a prime garden. Choose from those that have special assets: shelter, strength, texture, color, overhead excitement, magnificent detail or strange form. Search out and use those that can improve detail or strange form. Search out and use those that can improve your situation.

Once you are fully appreciative of trees, you can turn to the glories of shrubs, bulbs, perennials and annuals, grass and ground covers. All things living and growing will give vitality you can get in no other way. With these tools at hand, your goals are simple. All you must do is arrange a space between the soil and the sky.

Depending upon the plants you select you make aesthetic as well as visual decisions about your garden. Trees with leaves that are thinly cut provide shade that is only a few degrees cooler than the shining sun. But if you choose trees with huge, thick leaves you will have opaque shade and much cooler temperatures. By the very arrangement of our plants we create windbreaks or visual privacy to give us comfort for years, no matter the day or season.

A flowering ornamental crab prospers within a confined space beside a flight of steps. The box-like shape formed by railroad ties is softened by a break in the top line and a cluster of creeping plants.

Choose Carefully, Not Timidly

Each of us must make his or her own decisions. Some may want only the shelter of oaks or the privacy of pines, others a sampler garden with one of each kind so as to become acquainted with many trees.

Be careful in your choices, but daring. You needn't live with your mistakes. You can bury them or dig them up and ship them out. But nourish always the instinct in art to see the very heart of Nature. Find it in the line of a twig, the curl of a leaf or the thrust of an upward branch. Remember, gardening was intended as a patient art: we, as impatient gardeners, tend to hurry it.

Plants as sculptural ornaments

Many of the plants we know are truly sculptural ornaments, great masses and intriguing textures. Trees often qualify but perennial succulents serve as shining examples of the properties I have in mind. Succulents are a great, unrelated group having fine form. Their bold shapes spring from prehistoric hardships. When the land on which they grew changed slowly from moist to arid, the plants developed water-storing capabilities with fleshy leaves and fattened stems. Other varieties simply acquired drought-tolerant characteristics together with odd and exotic shapes.

But their prehistoric losses have been our horticultural gain. Their gross bodies and expandable trunks have made forms and patterns that are useful as ornamentation in our gardens. Cacti,

aloe, echeveria and sedum are all oddly dramatic. The spiny surfaces of cacti, the velvet-like texture of kalanchoe and the sharp, ribbon-like leaves of agave all deserve attention. In frost-free areas the Joshua tree and the saguaro grow to heroic size.

Elsewhere many must be potted and moved in and out as seasons change. Northerners do best with house plant specimens that vacation outdoors.

Find Drama in Native Plants

Consider the lessons to be learned here and apply them to dramatic plant material indigenous to your region. Spruce and pine may be trained to bonzai-like forms, fruit trees respond well to to-

piary pruning, but look for the plant that of itself offers orderly design and strange volumes.

The giant agave specimen shown here, *A. americana marginata,* has sharply pointed blades in bright green, and edged in white and cream. It stands alone in a seacoast garden, ornamenting an entry. Although I am a loyal Colorado gardener, I grudgingly admit that Californians have a flair for design with plants, on and beyond the merits of the exotic plants they have at their disposal. We have much to learn from these West Coast people.

Aloe varigata, Echeveria and *Asparagus plumosus* stand on a terrace in Balboa Park, San Diego, as in a sculptural museum.

A velvet-leafed *Kalanchoe beharensis* of the Crassula family has been allowed to grow its unbridled way toward sunlight. Its gardenmaker added bamboo stakes to support the plant when it appeared to be exceeding itself.

Plants with strong form and texture

Most plants are naturally graceful or distinguished, but there are certain trees—the twisted juniper, the paper mulberry and the giant live oak—that are things apart. They are magnificent show pieces that must be used where they stand. As we become aware of their importance we should clear a broad space around them so they may be viewed from every angle, much as you would a piece of sculpture. Think of them as living art objects of great value and provide them with dramatic approaches and suitable backdrops. The paper mulberry in the photograph is at Colonial Williamsburg.

Analyze your existing plants, their prime characteristics and their natural inclinations. Keep this information in mind as you introduce new plants so they do not compete with their forbears. Present your most distinguished plants with pride. They deserve all the consideration you can give.

Most gardeners are dreamers, living in the future and waiting for the day when the golden rain tree, *Koelreuteria,* blooms for the first time or the *Cotoneaster* shrubs will be thick enough to furnish streetside screening. They take less notice of the old peonies coming into fat bud, perhaps for the fiftieth or one hundredth time, as peonies are wont to do.

Count Present Blessings

We need to dream of the *now* of things as well as the wonders that are still to come. Instead of planting three crabapple shoots in separate holes, dig a wide, deep hole and plant all three together for a finer show a few years hence. Plant dogwood saplings, not in the center of the lawn but in front of a stand of dark pine or at the edge of a woodland so they can lean out into the sun as they do naturally.

Evaluate the quality of the leaves on your trees from the thin and semi-translucent quality of aspen, Liquidambar (known also as sweet gum) and maple, to the opaque quality of catalpa, magnolia and holly.

How Do the Branches Look?

Branching patterns are also a factor. The blue spruce gives dense shade in midsummer when the sun is high but allows the sun in winter between the widely separated layers of branches.

Locate your prized ornamental trees selfishly, where they will please you most. Leonardo Da Vinci was the first to record his pleasure in the luminosity of trees, particularly when they were planted between where he would be and the setting sun.

Consider too those trees with unusual linear patterns, the weeping and the corkscrew willows, the gnarled wisteria and the twisted pine. Their oddly-bent or jointed branches can give interest in summer and in winter.

Trees Work for Your Garden

A concentration of trees and shrubs can hide boundary fencing and make you scarcely aware of your garden's dimensions. Dappled shade can camouflage the slender strands of wire fencing and make you believe that your plot is without limits. A fine showing of flowering shrubs can claim so much attention that boundary markers go unnoticed. An adjacent view can be framed with evergreens and claimed as one's own.

If you have close neighbors whose house seems to loom over your land, plant evergreens—Austrian pine, Douglas fir or red cedar—to screen your view while maintaining ventilation. Deciduous trees will provide screening in summer but leave you open to view in winter.

Plants as small wonders

Among plants, trees are admittedly the largest and greatest living things we know, but strength and size aren't everything. At the opposite end of the scale we have other wonders, very small and extraordinary. In 'capsules' not much larger than those of miracle drugs we have the potential of roots, stems, leaves and flowers to brighten the dreariest spring.

To orchestrate a special springtime of your own, lay in an ample supply of bulbs in advance. Order them from your local supplier or a reputable mail order house and concentrate on flower colors that harmonize with each other and with your garden setting. Staying with lavender and yellow, the natural colors of spring, is perhaps the safest way. If you want more excitement select a combination of red and white with gold, or other hues more to your taste. If dissonance is more stimulating, look for all the extreme and clashing colors you can find, plant them out in the fall and then await their smashing performance.

Because these bulbs bloom from March through May in a little-to-big progression, it is

best to interweave your plantings so you have overlapping color and changing accents over a twelve week period. For an artful production, make a rough sketch of your grand plan before you reach for the spade or trowel.

If all is to go into one big bed, plant the late-blooming tulips in a prominent place, then the hyacinths, daffodils, and narcissi in adjacent clusters. Finally add the very early and very tiny squills (*Scilla*), crocus, snowdrops (*Galanthus*) and grape hyacinths (*Muscari*),

Clusters need not be equally spaced. I would reach for maximum sunlight and dodge the shade patterns of nearby trees. After turning the soil as well as I could without injuring existing perennials, I would dimple the ground where each bulb was to be planted and define clusters where the larger bulbs would go. Then I would scatter daffodils and crocus in drifts to fill the spaces between. Finally I would go over the entire bed with quantities of scilla and snowdrops, and perhaps some winter aconite near the front border as a preview showing. I would add casual plantings of bright blue grape hyacinth near the golden daffs and white narcissi to keep them pleasant company. Then to cap it all I would rhapsodize with a hundred or more crocus, starting near the tulip circles and moving forward. The crocus appear well before the tulips, competing with late snows for attention, covering the bare, cold ground. They persevere no matter how deep the snow and reappear, seemingly refreshed. As they fade and their blades ripen, the later shoots will disguise the scruffy leaves. (With all bulbs it is essential that the leaves be allowed to ripen at their own pace. This renews the bulb for bloom the following year. This is no place to trim and neaten the garden.)

If you still have a surplus, plant the extra small bulbs in the lawn nearby. Cut out a core of sod with a bulb planting tool, set a bulb or two and return the sod to its place as a cover. You may need to hold off on your first mowing in the spring to give the bulbs time to ripen fully.

Treat the Bulbs Well

Plant bulbs in late fall up to heavy frost. (Tulips planted too early may start growth during Indian summer.) Dig and turn the soil, smooth and set the bulbs down about one-and-a-quarter times their own height. Pack the soil lightly over them and add a winter cover of compost or leaf mold. Use no manure, it can burn the bulbs. In the spring a top dressing of dry manure can be added as the plants come into bud. Tulips and hyacinths are best lifted after flowering and ripening, for storage in a cool place in summer and replanting in the fall. Other bulbs can be left in the ground to improve and multiply through the years. In harsh climates deeper planting slows spring bloom and protects the plants from late heavy snows.

Buy quality bulbs and avoid stupendous offers as advertised in the Sunday supplements. Add a gathering of violets and spring 'forget-me-nots', *Anchusa myosotidiflora,* also known as *Brunnera macrophylla,* and have a grand spring show. Enjoy every minute of it, you're entitled.

Colonial Williamsburg's species tulips do well in a naturalized setting and against a dark background. Here *Tulipa Clusiana,* the candy striped red and white flower with a violet base, finds pleasant company with *Triteleia uniflora,* a sweet-scented, pale lilac beauty.

Plants for overhead excitement

Having a roof over one's head seems reassuring to humans, even in a garden. We do it to shade out the sun, to obscure a neighbor's view of us and to give ourselves the privacy we seem to crave. We use many devices—overhanging trees, patio covers and trailing vines. We look kindly on the designs of our forefathers who fashioned arbors, pergolas, allees and summerhouses, and use these concepts as our own. We grace these structures with clematis, wisteria, silver lace, jasmine and climbing roses for their glorious flowers and the sense of shelter they provide.

If you wish to screen a trellised porch but do not wish to give up a productive grapevine, cut a slit in the screening where the woody stems grow inward and then cover over the top of the rafters without disturbing the vine or its harvest. At the same time you will be protecting the fruit from the birds, but not from family predators.

Manmade Materials Can Serve

We also bow to the building materials of our own times, using durable plastics to keep out the rain while admitting warm light. We welcome the pattern of falling leaves to embellish utilitarian surfaces, to add random designs and pleasant color. In some instances a parasol may be all that is needed to temper the heat of the sun and you.

A roof grid and plastic panels were added to an entry area the better to shelter it from heavy rain. The rains came and the small leaves fell from the surrounding live oak trees. They fell on the roof plastic too and were allowed to remain because the patterns were more decorative than the plain sheeting.

For our own garden we have designed a white,

polyester awning from a former art object (Color Plate 28). The cloth was from a segment of Christo's Running Fence, that ribbon of beauty that rippled in the sun, a few summers ago, from Petaluma to the sea. We purchased an 18 x 60 foot section of the 'fence' from a rancher over whose land it traveled. The 18 x 18 foot awning we made from it is hooked to the fascia board of our house on one side and the terrace fence on the other. Ropes reach over notched posts that are eight feet high. They sway in the breeze, making the canopy responsive to wind currents and less likely to break away. It can go up or down in five minutes, and folds away into a blanket box.

A salvaged parachute can be tied to a hula hoop at the center hole and then lifted with a line between two tall trees. The perimeter lines can be tied to fence posts or stakes to shape the chute to an exciting architectural form. This is pretty enough to serve as focus for a garden wedding. It won't keep out heavy rain, but otherwise it is a real delight. You can dye it pink or paint it with big flowers.

Plants as design tools

There is no such thing as an insignificant plant. Closely examined, each is a miracle of engineering, production and self-perpetuation. If you can fulfill their needs as you would a child's, you and they can live well together. Be attentive to their needs, for yourself and for future generations, and they will reward you and serve you. The trees will provide privacy and seclusion, the shrubs screening and the flowers color. Together they distribute light and shade, modify the weather and please you with their intriguing bloom. If we arrange plants to stand apart, one from the other, they will bend in the wind and return your favors with rounded forms that highlight and backlight well.

If you do not treat them properly, they may stretch to seek the sun. They are capable of intent and do strange things. Some flowers bloom only when there is enough dew on their stalks to keep the ants from reaching their nectar. Others develop thorns, sticky discharges and strange smells to repel or tempt insects. Have respect for your plants if you wish to stay on good terms.

You Have a Wide Choice

Actually the dangers are few. Plants are so diverse that they would hardly join together to op-

pose you, and it is this diversity that is so valuable to the gardener. The holly and box make ideal hedgings, the lilac and spirea fine screening tools, the fruit trees graceful shade as well as tasty food. Pines and spruce set in a row make good windbreaks, and maple, ash and elm offer shade in summer and bare branches in winter to better admit the warming sun. Roses, iris and peonies bring fragrance and beauty. Oriental poppies and delphinium offer high drama. It is up to us to choose the right plant for each purpose.

Size and scale are vital considerations when choosing a plant, or for that matter a garden ornament. The tone of the item and its background are more important than you might expect. White lilies or a marble sculpture look best against filtered shade. Relative size is a continuous concern. As our gardens become smaller, so too should our flowers and plants. Giant tulips are wrong in a tiny dooryard garden. We have begun to miniaturize to good advantage. Delphiniums are getting shorter, intermediate iris are winning favor, but such changes don't come easily. Hybridizers have been striving for the biggest and the brightest for too long.

Miniaturization could be an advantage, even for growers. They would have less weight to lift and less to ship for the same profits. Right now miniature roses cost more that large ones, which seems ironic. Gardening is big business and it will get larger as other entertainment and travel costs zoom. If we want change we must speak out for it.

Outdoor Space Is an Investment

Landscape architects today suggest that we judge our garden projects on a cost-benefit ratio. With interior space running $30 to $40 per square foot versus $10 to $12 for outside living space, good terrace space can be a better investment than an addition to the kitchen or dining room. We all can manage with smaller rooms if we install floor-to-ceiling glass doors that give direct access to a patio or deck, or enlarge our views of outdoor living space. We can satisfy our psychological needs with lush foliage in concentrated garden areas. With exciting plants we can create an entirely different world. Closely-planted hedgings can give us greater privacy and absorb sounds of traffic that would otherwise intrude.

Enjoy the special wonder of asparagus fern as the light falls on it in early winter. Corseted within a wire frame, the mature plant shown, its

Euonymus, woodbine or bittersweet to cancel out the forbidding look.

If you have an old apple tree that you deeply love, support its tired branches with a crutch made from a limb discard. You may add several years to the tree and get Brownie points for your concern.

With one vigorous rose climber and a barrel hoop, mark a gateway into a garden. Wrap the strap iron with a bit of dark-coated wire to give the plant an easier purchase.

Shape a parterre garden with boxwood hedging and plant the center spaces with anemones, pansies and English daisies. Lay brick walkways and edge these with star-of-Bethlehem, *Ornithogalum,* for a spring show. This Colonial design at Williamsburg portrays the British flag.

fibrous stems and frothy tips, survives the buffeting winds and icy rains to give pleasure once again when we need it most. This after a generous springtime offering of succulent and tasty asparagus tips and a summer of ferny green and the easy production of viable seeds for another valuable planting.

Residential landscaping with native and apt plants can give a cohesiveness to a neighborhood, even when the houses vary widely in appearance. Good plantings add to the value of a property; they can screen architectural mistakes and complement good design. With the help of trees it is possible to reduce fuel and air-conditioning costs, shading a house in summer and buffering against harsh winds in winter. Evergreens provide us with cooling views and tall trees give a lift to the breezes and draw away stagnant air.

Embellish Bare Fences

Dwarf fruit trees can be planted beside a boundary fence and trimmed front and back so the remaining branches spread like a fan. Chain-link fencing begs to be clothed. Try creeping

Plants for closer viewing

Spend an entire day with your eyes focused for close-up viewing. Stoop down to gaze into the vaulted chamber of a tall, bearded iris flower. Examine the well-ordered spiral design of a giant sunflower seedhead. Inspect the fine structuring and placement of tiny flowers on the golden Achillea stalk. In each instance the detailing is so exquisite it will put you in awe of its master designer. Do homage, at least for the day, to the astonishments and bewilderments around you. Gape and admire, stare and marvel. Be duly impressed with all the wonderments found in gardening. Enjoy your privileges.

Tie fuchsia to a bamboo screen close by your favorite garden chair and enjoy the development of each new bud and bloom. Or grow tomatoes, eggplant, sugarsnap peas or cucumbers in a similar fashion.

Use All the Senses

Gardening, to my way of thinking, should be first and foremost a gratifying experience. It should include introspection and close inspection. It should exercise our eyes, our sense of smell and sense of touch, and be both escape and rejuvenation. It should encourage us to enjoy the shadows of ferns on a patio wall, the aerial strength of baby's breath, *Gypsophila,* as it stands poised over other flowers. It should stop us in our tracks to bend down and touch the cushion softness of a clump of sedum.

When we see for the first time a robust stand of *Tithonia,* we should walk up to the blooms of this Mexican sunflower and get acquainted by examining the petals and stamens, and study the jointing of this fast-growing annual.

When a gardener hangs baskets of pendulous begonias under the wide eaves of her house, start a conversation with her and praise her for her enterprise. Whether your delights are color, shape or scent pursue your preferences with the same vigor you would a session of tree-trimming, otherwise you'll miss much.

Entice Others

Once you are convinced of the value of magnifying your pleasures, create situations in which your family members or guests might be caught in the trap. Grow vegetables in containers on your terrace so you can keep watch on the eggplants as they turn to a gleaming purple-blue and the rhubarb chard to a rosy red.

If you have no garden space, grow potted plants on a balcony or a roof. With a limited selection you will get to know your petunias better and faster than you might on a half-acre plot.

If you live in a mild area grow a double row of *Agapanthus* across your front line as an early summer display. If you have a white house, choose blue flowers; white blooms with warm earth colors.

Converse with your plants in the morning as you snap off the faded blooms of iris and day lily. Stop to admire your blue flax during the early hours because they will be wilting by afternoon to make way for the next day's crop.

For a longer look, grow everlastings in the garden for drying later. Try globe amaranth, *Gomphrena globosa,* one of the most useful blooms, and *Helichrysum bracteatum,* the popular strawflower.

Go medieval if you dare and cut a place for turf seats in a hillside. Then cut meadow sod three to

four inches deep and use it as cushions for your benches. Select sod that is laced with tiny wildflowers and sit on one part while you study the flowers in the other.

Let the Plants Guide You

Look more closely at your perennials and work for happier combinations. Grow *Veronica* with white *Physostegia,* wild carrot with *Rudbeckia,* chrysanthemums in front of hollyhocks, and white phlox with golden glow *Rudbeckia laciniata*. Try blue *Scabiosa* in front of cosmos and annual asters with Michaelmas daisies. Use white flowers like green foliage as a means of separating uncomfortable color combinations.

You can plant your perennial garden with careful spacing between plants so they will look right ten years from now or you can plant for earlier maturity and admit that you will need to make changes in the next ten years. A decade is too long for me. Plants grow, some die, you change and your neighborhood changes. For an easier career, learn to adjust.

For the Long Run

If you would like to become better acquainted with evergreens you might try starting a small pinetum. This would be a collection of pines and other conifers to tend while they grew. It might take ten years before you would have specimens to show and twenty-five years before you would have a collection worthy of attention. In the meantime you would learn the subtle differences between these needled trees. The knowledge could extend from your life to that of your grandchildren. While the pinetum is developing you can use the land between the seedlings for other projects.

Plants shaped to your liking

With plant materials we have an awesome responsibility. We are at liberty to grow them to shapes and lines they would follow naturally or bend, prune or cut them to forms of our own devising. While we are becoming acquainted with our stock, we would better give trees and shrubs the freedom to reveal their natural tendencies before we dare to inflict them with our own ideas and friviolities. It is not so much a matter of offending a particular plant as it is learning how much rigidity or flexibility a plant has, how thick its foliage grows, or how well it survives drastic pruning.

Topiary is a strange garden discipline, perhaps intended to prove that the gardener has control over his fast-growing evergreen forms. Alexander Pope was against it. ''We shape trees in the most awkward forms of men and animals rather than the most regular of their own.''

Prune for Overall Design

Nevertheless there are fine opportunities for the decoration of a garden in judicious pruning of certain trees and shrubs. Cypress, privet, yew, box and holly all lend themselves to disciplined forms. For the gardener it takes wire and stakes, together with patient clipping. The tendency today is away from elaborate and whimsical

forms that were first intended to replace marble statues as an economy measure. These droll shapes of birds and beasts are still maintained in England, primarily to amuse the tourists, and to retain the old ways.

In the best tradition, Colonial Williamsburg's gardeners have shaped a holly tree to a layered cone. Box hedging encircles the tree and adjacent beds.

Nowadays a well-trimmed tree hedge is the most we seem to undertake. We claim a labor shortage although we have power equipment that does work three or four times faster than the hand-powered gardener is able to. A tree hedge of evergreen stock decorates this home in downtown San Francisco. It occupies little space and lends distinction.

Bend a Tree to your Will

In Tudor times hedges were grown wide and tall and pruned with openings deep enough to give shelter when the rains came. Trees were planted close together to create walled corridors. Some, when young, were bent toward each other to form a tunnel corridor of green. When a variety of plants was used the hedges assumed a tapestry effect. Here saplings line a crosscorridor and are bent as they grow to interlace above. Lightweight lathing and heavy wire help with the training.

Topiary allows the gardener to work in a limited space and to control size. In a formal setting it can give importance to a plant. Experts advise using rope instead of wire and shaping the plants in spring when the stems are tender. If the art isn't great, it at least takes horticultural skill. Birds and animals may be out, but the layered look seen at Colonial Williamsburg is in. And we can always do what the Romans did—take the fragrant clippings indoors to freshen the air.

In our own life and times we can train a spreading tree into an umbrella shape. An evergreen pear, trimmed upward and flattened on the top, makes a delightful shelter in mild climates. A standard apple should serve as well in temperate climes. In the illustration, a pear is espaliered along fence posts for easy pickings at the Williamsburg Restoration. Neighboring dogwood announces the arrival of spring.

We can still emulate the Elizabethans and shape hedged enclosures hung with roses or jasmine. We can make the paths waterproof by building them on a sandy base and covering this with paving stones. In the center we can grow sod thick enough to wiggle our toes in.

Plants shaped by Nature

If you want a garden of great beauty, select plants that have space to grow to their natural height and width. Choose trees of great strength that barely bend in the wind. Learn how these familar plants give stability to our lives as well as our gardens. Allow each shrub to develop according to its particular habits and form an individual mass. All this unbridled growing may make your plot look rank, but remember that Nature isn't ever tidy.

Grow native plants where you can, but understand what is native. A shrub brought down from a hillside ravine a few miles from your raw land will be a struggling immigrant in need of help. If you hope to assist, try to duplicate the conditions the plant enjoyed in its original setting. Bring in some of the original soil and provide a like amount of shade and moisture. Even native gardening isn't easy.

Aspen is the exception that proves the rule. They have been brought down from the mountains to grow well in Illinois and Tennessee. The roots of the aspen travel horizontally and close to the surface. Once a small grove of saplings is es-tablished it can be extended by loosening the soil around the grove's perimeter where you want other volunteers. Lateral roots will send up new shoots.

Tame the Wild Judiciously

If you are starting with overgrown ground, cut a path through the brambles to a small retreat. Clothe the ground with small flowers and fill the moist crevices with young ferns. Thin out some of the tangled shrubbery to give you a longer view and cut an opening in the high branches so you can feel the sun on your shoulders. Domesticate only so much as seems necessary for your personal comfort. Make your 'improvements' so carefully that they are not evident.

Before you plant a tree, recognize what kind of shade it will provide: light, feathery interruptions of the sun, as with the locust and mimosa, or broad, overlapping layers of shade as with the oak or hickory. Green ash, linden and fruit trees offer something in between.

A fine tree gives a gentle rhythm to a garden. It moves gently in a kindly breeze and adds elements of great excitement when a storm blows in.

Push Your Horizons Out

We need to extend the walls of our lives; we have lived too long in cubical spaces. We need soft edges and wiggly lines. Alan Watts said that "Nature is wiggly and so are we. Our brains are wiggly too. Birds, leaves and trees live together in a network. Everything is interconnected. We do not understand because a part cannot comprehend the whole."

Nan Fairbrother, an English horticulturist, was more reassuring. She wrote, "When one realizes that we, as puny animals, dominate this world by the force of our spirit, we should be able to design gardens with flair and beauty."

Investigate the Habitat

Before you start a new garden take walks in the wild areas nearby and make notes of the deciduous and evergreen plants that grow there naturally. Study their color range and textures and then take your findings to the local nursery center and purchase these plants to arrange in similar ways. The costs of these natives should be less than plants shipped in from other areas.

The common sunflower *Helianthus annuus* is one of sixty species that are an integral part of our native environment. It grows twelve feet high with twelve-inch flowers. For a dramatic touch, plant them in a double row on the north edge of your vegetable garden.

Realize that no region has such dependable rainfall that you can plant and walk away. Success with plants depends on caretaking, sometimes for years to come. When some of them overgrow their prescribed space, move them elsewhere where their volume can be tolerated, or failing that, give them away to an aspiring gardenmaker.

Design for Harmony

As you design, avoid inharmonious groupings as you would with people. Aspire to quiet, restful forms and let the busy ornamental trees stand near their shade. Color differences should be subtle, not bold. A painter arranges his harmonies so they flow, one to another, with soft greys dappled in between. Position purple beech and red maple with care and use no more than a few. As seasons change, so too our standards. Fall color knows no bounds and follows few rules. It intensifies everything around.

In some seasons the color of the bark or the fruit is as important as the color of the leaves. Keep this in mind when you are making value judgments.

Shrubs are too often selected for the color of their bloom, which is certainly a fleeting factor. Lilacs, *Syringa,* mock orange, *Philadelphus,* and bridal wreath, *Spiraea prunifolia plena* and *S. Vanhouttei* bloom for two to three weeks in spring. Decisions are better made on texture and shape.

With most plant material, the question persists. Is immediate or long-term beauty most valuable? A spindly, rare specimen that takes twenty years to mature may have less value to you than an ordinary tree that grows fast and contributes to your garden during all of those twenty years. Evaluate all that is available and make your own decisions.

The saguaro cactus, *Carnegiea gigantea,* is a giant in any desert garden. The largest specimens in the world grow in southern Arizona on the Sonoran desert; this specimen is at the Sonora Desert Museum in Tucson. They grow naturally to sixty feet high with a post-like body and candelabra arms. In some instances the flowering tips become fasciated—a widening of the flowering stalk. This is an ornament that Nature produces unassisted.

Plants as small conceits

Start modestly. If all you know how to grow is morning glories, do that with a flair. Build a cage big enough for a few people to sit in and plant morning glories at the base of each supporting post. When the vines climb up and begin to bloom have a breakfast party and invite your friends to help you celebrate the first blooming.

If you have never had an knack with these vines perhaps you have been too kind to them. Good, rich soil is a waste; they prefer ordinary soil and perform best along some alley fence where they can greet the sun at dawn. You can hurry their sprouting further by nicking the hard seed coat with a knife or by allowing the seed to soak overnight before planting. You can also shake them (dry) in a jar lined with sandpaper to thin the husk.

Knots, Parterres and Mazes

Go historic and build a knot garden according to ancient design. Intertwine low-growing herbs— sage, basil, balm, rosemary, thyme, and pennyroyal in meandering rows. Add fennel or tarragon as a centerpiece or install a modest sundial. Don't make it too fancy; Francis Bacon complained that some knots were so intricate they looked like baked tarts.

Consider doing a parterre garden of many symmetrical parts. Lay paths between and edge the planting beds with small hedgings or other edgings. What you can't plant immediately, cover with colored sand or stone. Most parterres are on land but if you have a pool you might pattern the bottom before you fill it with water.

Do a maze with zigzag paths, a labyrinth on a spiral route, or build a mount on a high point of land where you can survey your entire domain.

Fool the Eye

If you have a long narrow lot, strive for optical deception. Add hedge wings and shrub groupings out from the boundaries to slow the headlong race to the back line. Prune tall plants downward so they spread sideways instead. Extend partitions out from the side fencing, past the center point, so that visitors are required to wind their way into terrace spaces. Groom existing trees that grow near your side boundaries even though their branches extend over neighboring property. They will strengthen the illusion that your lot is wider.

To soften the lines of a stately stair add evergreen vines close to the risers. Keep it well-trimmed for safety.

Where the ground is poor and the rocks are many, grow Iceland poppies. Add some twisted juniper to silhouette the blooms.

A man from Harlingen trimmed a creeping fig vine to the shape of his favorite state. You might do the same with yours. It would be a square thing to do in Colorado.

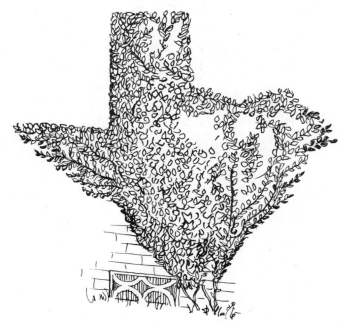

Plants as personal triumphs

Let each of us plant what pleases us most and be sensitive to what our minds and hearts tell us. Work always to embellish rather than fill a plot. As with the painting of landscapes, the neutral areas between are important too.

Take heed of the Sesame Street children as they sing "I believe in miracles, like honeycombs and flowers"—and choose your own wonders.

Work always to improve your plants and your garden, but don't ever make things final. Continue to keep the gate open to new encounters. Delve into the shape of trees and shrubs, study circles, squares and triangles and determine which you are most comfortable with.

Take a long look at the soft and sinuous line. Reshape your grounds to a graceful curve on a water-holding contour. If the need for a lawn is strong, plant it to a circle form on a square plot or an oval to a rectangle. Rounded forms make the mowing easier and leave space for flower beds of varying depths.

Decide early what kind of lawn you wish to have—rich green and pool-table smooth, short-cropped and mostly weeds, or star-spangled green interrupted by hundreds of small flowers. Each depends on how much energy you are willing to put into it.

Build yourself a secret garden in a place hidden behind shrubs and small trees. Make access difficult and exclusive. Protect it as a world apart, where you may sit and dream without interruption.

Container Gardens

Create a lush container garden on a bare concrete slab. Fill buckets and pots with robust annuals, any of the big four, petunias, marigolds, zinnias and snaps. Or try pot-grown vegetables, cucumbers and eggplants, that climb small trellises. If you are shy of containers, lay bags of rich soil on the concrete and slit them open wide enough to accept starts of tomatoes or seeds of carrots and sugarsnap peas. If you think container planting is new, think again. Pliny recommended it to the Greeks twenty centuries ago. He suggested the use of old baskets for moving plants about.

If you love fruit, grow a wall orchard along the sunny side of your terrace. Trim two or three varieties to fan against the wall and then plant others on the opposite side ten feet out from the terrace for a larger crop and added privacy. *Espalier,* should you be interested, is a French word coming from epaulet and alluding to the branches, trained at right angles to the stem.

Green the Desert—Modestly

If you live in a desert but crave the company of plants, roof the space between your house and garage, and plant *Potentilla* and needled evergreen shrubs under it in planting pockets lined with polyethylene plastic bags. and filled with garden loam. Arrange a few handsome boulders and cover the remaining soil with polished river pebbles. Water the plants in the evening and moisten the area with a fine mist in the morning for daytime cooling.

We have several tall spruce in our garden, including one forty-footer on which the branches bow down to the ground. We use the 20-foot circle as a cool summerhouse and identify it as our moose nest tree. In the high mountains moose look for such trees as winter shelter. As snows build up the tree becomes a green igloo. A narrow passage between the branches on the leeward side provides air and access.

Artist-Gardeners, Gardener-Artists

Some gardeners think of themselves as theatrical directors. One planted his best pink hollyhocks in the center of a small Taos courtyard. No matter where one stood the *Althaea rosea* was in bright sunlight against a dark background. Another welcomes spring with golden forsythia shrubs, some on the east side of the garden for morning backlighting and a larger group to the west beside a white rail fence.

Another artist planted a Sunburst locust in front of a grey-green house. The chartreuse effect is startling in spring and mellow in fall. In midsummer the hot sun is tempered by the plant's cool emerald-green leaves. Still another designed a pond garden by rerouting a mountain stream. He planted it with bog plants and water hyacinths and stocked it with trout fingerlings that swam to the edge of the deck to beg for dried dog food from his own hand. He built a small bridge and cut a path that encircles the water through a meadow of wildflowers.

West Coast gardeners filled an entire plot with

small white flowers I could not identify. They could be *Mesembryanthemum lineare,* the fig marigold, or a strain of *Anemone blanda,* the Grecian windflower. I have trouble with California plants.

Few of us take the time to design an urn for a particular plant as has this artisan for an *Agave.*

In the long run, trees are our greatest treasure. We may have a great year when our delphiniums soar seven feet high in great spires of bloom, or our *Euonymus americanus* or burning bush will give forth flaming color on an autumn day, but these triumphs will fade with the years and only fine trees will grow from one generation to the next. Each region of the country has its own giants: great maples, hickories, magnolias, lindens, and beech. Our trees make our gardens, they frame, they shade and they shelter us. They establish our garden traditions.

As evidence of their importance allow me to cite several examples among the color plates in this volume. The scrub oak, *Quercus ilicifolia,* shown in Color Plate 2, is of modest height, but enduring. It gives substance to the land, grows slowly, but clothes the countryside for generations. The live oak, *Quercus chrysolepis,* shown in Plates 26 and 27 grows best from Oregon to lower California. It is an evergreen tree that grows fifty to eighty feet high and is a source of great pride in the far west.

The Colorado blue spruce, *Picea pungens,* is a beautiful evergreen, hardy from our Canadian boundary southward. The trees are as varied in coloring as cousins. A fistful of seedlings acquired from the United States Forestry Service nursery can vary through several shades of green into a true blue. Experts are always on the lookout for real glisteners, in a silvery blue. A landscape architect of our acquaintance retired comfortably as a supplier of blue spruce and true-blue columbine. Together they made a fine sinecure.

Spruce serve to pillar a garden. They should not be set too close to a house or they will become distorted as they grow. For small scale gardens, the spruce candles should be nipped each year to lessen growth. This fine tree makes an excellent backdrop for flowers and shrubs. It even serves well for smaller groupings, as with the cacti shown in Color Plate 13.

Russian olive, *Elaeagnus angustifolia,* is of a family of trees and shrubs having edible and decorative fruits. It has silver-grey leaves and small yellow flowers in spring. It is spiny and weedy but still loved by some. It can be trimmed from shrub to tree by a caring gardener, and will grow into a tree of strong character. An example is the specimen shown in Color Plate 8.

Big and Little Apples

Apple trees are a boon to any designer. The ancient specimens are gnarled and spreading, offering magnificent bloom in spring before the leaves grow full, dense shade in summer, bountiful fruit in early fall for eating straight, cooking to a sauce or jelly, or drying in the sun for winter use.

Dwarf trees that grow eight to ten feet high and semi-dwarfs at twelve to fifteen feet are ideal for the gardener short on space. The mature dwarfs shown in Color Plate 25 are fine accents in an entry garden, decorative in every season— including winter, when their branches cradle heavy snows.

Some three centuries ago, John Gerard, the medieval herbalist, wondered why gardeners "looke dangerously up at Planets, that might safely looke down at Plants." The question is more appropriate now than before.

CHAPTER THREE

Structures

If you can build a doghouse you should be able to construct other valuable and useful items for your garden. If you have the desire to do so, you will learn automatically. It may not be an overnight revelation but it will come in easy stages. In time you should be able to saw a straight edge and nail a board without bending the nail or denting the lumber. Also there is exhilaration in doing things you previously had to hire out.

Start with a bench, then make a fence, and do each as well as you are able. Resolve, on paper, any questions on framing and finishing. Figure materials needed, and costs. Make a list and take it to your local building supply center. The people there should welcome your business and be willing to cut special boards to order—for a fee—should you not have the skill or the equipment to cut them yourself. Once acquainted with the services available, you should be ready to move on to bigger and better undertakings.

If it seems practical, make your next project a his-and-her affair, particularly if it needs a combination of wild imagination and practical talents. Fight out your differences over a scratch pad with two pencils. Sketching, no matter how inept, clarifies ideas, and double input makes for better family solutions.

Don't Stop with a Fence

Keep the momentum going, if it feels good, by tackling a more creative venture—a fancy pergola, a special baffle or a comfortable reading platform. Set the tone, the mood or the style you wish to project. Improve your level of craftsmanship as you go. Change your classification from wood butcher to cabinetmaker. Seldom can construction be too precise or too prim. The elements work their ways quickly on new construction, adding the weathered look long before you want it.

Adequate foundations are essential in every project but a floating ornament. Otherwise, fence posts will soon start to lean from the heaving and settling of soil. A gazebo merely set on a frame on the ground will assume a rakish tilt in short order. Stone paths and brick terraces need a sand-packed base for quick drainage and to keep the surface uniform. Quality materials help make quality products, but sometimes salvaged materials have more quality than new.

Used Can Be Useful

Shop secondhand lumber yards, explore junkyards. Be alert to the razing of old houses. You may be able to pick up some solid, redwood porch columns for a song and make a fine pergola with them. Be of open mind to any opportunities. You really can't tell what you want until you see it. Who would have thought that a bundle of old mirrors would be just right to line the back wall of your party shed? They can double the room's size and the number of people attending, and at the same time reflect all the bright colors in your garden.

Enlist the services of your family early if you plan to build many fences. You will need helpers—wife, husband, son or daughter—to hold the boards true while you nail, and to check the levelness of your framing. Don't underrate the power of teenage muscles. They are very strong and can be helpful in holding a gasoline-powered posthole digger in place. Most rental posthole equipment takes at least two people to keep it from going in all directions.

Materials Should Be Appropriate

If you are reproducing a historical design, use quality lumber and suitable metalwork wherever possible. Search out a metalsmith to do custom hinges and latches in keeping with the design, to capture the element of authenticity. Then seek to reinforce the ambience you have created with old-world flowers, shrubs and trees. Use these structures as they were first intended and then work to adapt them to your uses.

If you prefer to work in the contemporary idiom, fashion strange gates and unfamiliar garden seats for use, and for the pleasure to be found in the making. As one of today's craftsmen, be liberated. Do what you choose and allow few inhibitions to prevail.

Those who dare their own designs get mixed results. Some are real triumphs, and only a few are true disasters. The pursuit of the structural arts can be a fine excursion for anyone. Even the unskilled among us should enjoy the involvement and be happy with their lot. Try to curb your enthusiasms to the extent that your designs fit into the existing character of your neighborhood. Make your design decisions to blend with the physical features of the land and the inclinations of your neighbors.

If the neighborhood doesn't come up to your expectations, do a little quiet campaigning. If you wish to plant trees along your rear property line for greater privacy and to develop 'forest coolness', talk it up around the block, and find out where you could buy trees for everyone, at a discount. The same system can prevail with uniform boundary fences or parkway trees. Since the neighborhood often affects the value of a home, group projects can be of benefit to all.

Building Can Spark Improvements

The building of a new gate, a summerhouse down in the ravine, or a new roof over the rear terrace can be a stimulating venture for the most plant-oriented gardener. It gives him new reason to rearrange the perennial beds, to plant that wisteria vine out front, or to begin training the weeping crab in the rear forty to an umbrella shape to give shade for morning visitors.

These are mostly theories and broad generalities but the specifics that follow are intended to trap you further. I hope the ideas offered will provide assurance and reinforcement as you pursue your own creative instincts.

One ambitious gardener built an arched entry and fence to hold a magnificent Wisteria vine and then added a gate and painted it in a greyed purple to match the color of the blossoms.

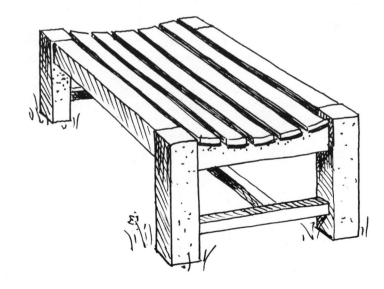

Gates that welcome

Well designed, a gate is a modest investment, a genuine pleasure and a great clue to the disposition of its owner and to the kind of garden it gives access to. It is a point beyond which people do not go, except by invitation. It serves as a symbol of hospitality but is contradictory in nature, welcoming a special few and turning away all others.

Perhaps because of their various meanings, gates are widely diverse. They present friendly or hostile facades. Some are plainly utilitarian—to keep the kids out or the dogs in.

It is time for clarification. It is time to design more gates that express their intent, more that are hospitable and more that welcome strangers.

More and Better Gates

With all these theories to be advanced, and a few problems on ventilation, control and privacy to be solved, it is apparent that we should be designing more and better gates. It is time for the artists among us to accept the challenge and create new solutions.

Gates are a great opportunity. With a pair of hinges and the right lumber, we can design a rococo number, elaborate in nature and delicate in appearance. We can reveal our conservatism with a design that seems to exude dignity, or uncover a frivolous aspect we didn't know we had. There are colorful designs that incorporate the owner's house numbers in the assemblage; the best ones show the numbers clearly enough to be helpful to the substitute mail carrier.

Good Construction Essential

No matter the message, the gate itself must be well-constructed. To make sure that it is flat and square, assemble the gate panel on a big work table or the floor. Set the gate posts first, in concrete and precisely upright. Then measure the precise space between, top and bottom, before you make final cuts on the gate itself. It doesn't pay to discover that the gate and its hinges are two inches too wide for the space specified. If the gate is thick, leave extra room for clearance as it swings. Construct it with diagonal reinforcements. With nothing but side support, it will want to sag. Select or make a good latch and add a hidden screen door hook for inside use when you leave town.

The multi-layered Brownsville gate is as big

and sturdy as Texas. It is built of cross-lathing with an inner and outer frame. It speaks of old-world Victorianism and shows its age. Six-inch rods, capped with cast-iron flowers or cupids, hold it all together. Children of past generations must have used the bottom board as a toe-hold for swinging, because the latch side now drags on the brick paving. Still there is stability, four-square, in this elegant design. I admit that it looks a bit heavy-handed, but I like it.

A slot gate on Carmel Point admits cool breezes without sacrificing privacy. Top-quality redwood in 1″ x 4″ strips are mounted within a reinforced 2″ x 6″ frame. The strips are separated from each other by 1″ x 4″ spacers, each two inches high. The gate and its fence, because of its thickness, offers passersby the thinnest possible glimpses of the garden's interior. Monterey pines loom overhead and ivy climbs the fencing. The garden, with its six-foot-high walls, seems a private room, richly endowed.

The slot gate with its latch is a fine example of extraordinary workmanship. The latch is all of wood. The protruding rod slides the back bolt into a slot in the door jamb. The front bolt serves as a fixed stopper which prevents the gate from swinging through. The gate frame is notched to accommodate the front and back latch plates. All

fittings and spacings are precise and beautiful.

The split-door entry shown in Color Plate 1 is actually an inner gate to a private garden space. At night the door is closed and the area softly lighted to be enjoyed when viewed through the uncurtained living room windows. The split door, which stands between the garage and the front wing of the house, can be opened wide, half-closed to deflect strong winds, or shut tight for complete privacy. A bougainvillea vine climbs the left side to a trellis that spans the portal, and two Podocarpus shrubs stand in double-stacked and weighted tubs on the other side. Coral bells, *Heuchera sanguinea,* fill the front corner, and tuberous begonias and camellias color the inner space. Live oaks shelter overhead.

Protect your creation with weather-resistant paints or stains to keep it beautiful. If your design includes a low cross board that might tempt youngsters to swing upon it, either change the design or make the hinge-gatepost taller to hold a diagonal support of strong wire.

Some theorize that a gate should lean slightly toward its closing position so it never stands ajar. It's not a bad theory but it generates a lot of banging which could get on your nerves if the gate is beside your kitchen door.

Gates that tempt and invite

"For too long the front yard has been an image builder, an expensive plot of ground that by tradition has related more to our neighbors than to ourselves." So said David F. Jones, landscape architect, who is intent on recapturing this land for personal use. Chris Moritz, another landscape architect, claims we need to get gardeners into political offices, mortgage companies and banks to influence ordinance on gates, fencing, and set-backs, so we can make better use of our garden spaces.

If you are contemplating lotline-to-lotline use of limited space check first with your local government on existing ordinances. If you think they treat you unfairly, make a case of it and see if you can gather the help of others of like mind, to change the system. A walled front garden can add to your family's living space, ease housework and foster better health. It can reduce the noise and smell of automobiles, protect your children from traffic hazards and give them a play area they can claim as their own.

Dooryards a Pleasure

Neighbors who at first may be offended by your reach to the front sidewalk should soon realize

the value of new and controlled outdoor space. Once you have pioneered the theory, they may well imitate your move to the front line.

There are energy-saving aspects to the door-yard garden. Fenced and gated, the front yard becomes secure. You can open doors and windows and leave them open through the day. As long as the air flows freely, the need for summer air-conditioning is lessened. If your house faces south you can use the courtyard in winter as the site for a midday picnic and save on the gasoline you would have used riding out into the country. We all need to become more self-sufficient, but we don't want to do it stingily. We can, with a little planning, be more self-reliant, but we would like to do it with gusto and a flair. The gates and fences we create are part of the grand scheme.

Some define their domain on a hillside with a handsome gate and wire to either side in the shrubbery. This Mill Valley gardener suggests an open-gate policy but the design and embellishments are so fine that few uninvited guests would dare to intrude. Halfway up the stairway there is a waiting bench where, according to Japanese tradition, guests should linger until they are summoned further. The garden appears wild but ivy and fern clothe the site and the tree branches are nicely trimmed, showing evidence of continued care.

The perforated ceramic panels framed within the well-designed portal glisten in the sunlight. The steps are a series of small plateaus, some framed with four-by-sixes, other with native stone.

As in all aspects of garden art, it is a matter of taste and discernment. The right gate for the right fence still needs to be related to the right house. It is the solutions that count, not the cost of the project.

The photo opposite shows a simple design of excellent proportions. The lattice work in the upper panel is precisely determined so the lath strips cross at the same interval in each corner. The lamp on the gatepost is of good design and counterbalances the small panel on the gate that holds the latch rod. An extra molding hides the nails in the grapestake strips used in the lowest panel.

A thick hedge has been grown on either side of a wire fence completely hiding its utilitarian appearance. At the same time the wire fence back-

bone makes the hedging almost impenetrable.

As further evidence of quality construction, the gate sill is made of concrete, assuring that the gateposts will remain upright and the space between fixed.

Craftsman or artist, the maker of this double gate has a taste for the frivolous. Starting with the secondhand frames of two narrow doors he has removed the inner panels and replaced them with stick figures made of reinforcing rods. The symbols of man, woman, sun, tree and deer seem to tell it all in Aspen, Colorado. The courtyard offers a sandpile for the children, a fireplace for cookouts and a flagstone and pebbled surface underfoot. It suggests casual living at its best in a brick cottage from mining camp days. Christmas tree lights still light the way in midsummer and will be ready to go when the next skiing season begins. Before the snows get too deep the gates will need to be swung open to serve as side panels at the entry. The stick figures will then define themselves well against the bright snow.

Gates and more gates

One would think that after you have seen a few gates you had seen them all, but this is not true. The possibilities are infinite. Each of us brings his or her own eccentricities to the problem, and when the next generation of gardeners are born there will be that many more potential variations.

Traditional Designs

If you favor historical and traditional designs, you are in luck. Each section of the country has its own treasures: Sturbridge Village in Massachusetts; Greenfield Village in Michigan; Cantigny in Illinois, and Filoli in California. But if you want to see the maximum variety of gates, go to Colonial Williamsburg in Virginia. If you can schedule a vacation at the same time, take in their Garden Symposium in March or April. The opportunity is exceptional. In addition to lectures and discussions you can witness a hundred small Colonial gardens as they all come into bloom about the same time.

If you choose to study the matter further, take a swing down through the Carolinas and Georgia to see the great gardens of the South. Tour the plantation gardens at Orton, the Tryon Palace at New Bern, and the small private gardens in Old Charleston. See the great historical gardens at Magnolia and Middleton. Stop off at the Callaway Gardens at Pine Mountain, Georgia, and the Bel-

lingrath Gardens in Mississippi. Walk through the French Quarter in New Orleans with head high to better view the balcony gardens of that old settlement. Drive past the old cemeteries to Longue Vue Gardens and continue north on the Natchez Trail, visiting plantation gardens along the way. Move on to Memphis and the Botanical Gardens there and across and up the river to the Missouri Botanical in St. Louis. Or ride on into Chicago and this city's Botanical Gardens near Skokie, and the Morton Arboretum near Lisle.

Garden Pleasures Everywhere

In each place you will find flowers and find plants in great abundance, and gates and fences to study and enjoy. The circle tour described above is just one of many you might undertake in other parts of our continent. Each journey suggests new plant material and new structures.

Sketch a Few Possibilities

If it is gates and only gates that interest you now, recall those you have liked in the past and those you see here. Get out your sketch pad and quickly rough out ten possibilities. Then show the sketches to your family. Based on their comments, rework the favored designs and add landscape touches, the fence, the shrub, or the tree in your garden that this gate would stand next to. If the gate under consideration is six feet high and the shrub three, draw them to scale. Then stand your sketches on a table or counter where you will see them often and unexpectedly. This is the best way to evaluate an idea quickly. If, after a week, the project is still in the doldrums, discard your sketches and start over again.

The two gates shown on these pages reflect the same kind of superb craftsmanship we associate with Colonial design. The light-colored gate is from one of the ten faculty gardens on the campus of the University of Virginia at Charlottesville. The double maroon gate is from Colonial Williamsburg, 125 miles away.

Each is a beautiful understatement, showing fine carpentry, curved forms and practical height and width. The brick walls that flank each gate are neatly and expertly laid up with scored mortar joints and appropriate caps. The gateposts are specifically designed for their gate and serve as a graceful transition between brick and wood.

The beaded paneling on the Charlottesville gate

suggests a pinwheel pattern on the lower half. The curved top is capped with metal and painted to protect it somewhat from the weather.

The dark Williamsburg gate has a mitred look from the square spokes to the diamond inserts. The bottom edge is uneven.

Both gates indicate the work of master craftsmen; still a zealous amateur could copy these designs as a winter project in the family workshop. It wouldn't be easy, but it could be done. Building the brick walls is another matter.

The jointing of a split door (shown in Color Plate 1) looks complicated, but needn't be. You start with a solid door but you don't attempt to cut a zigzag joint. Instead you cut the door in half at a determined height and notch downward an inch on the bottom half and upward on the top half. You lose an inch on the height of the finished door but you should have a neat joint. Put your latching mechanism on the lower half of the door and a slide bolt on the top half to join the parts together when you choose. A split door gives you ventilation while retaining a gate barrier, or a solid door against weather or intruders, when you need it.

Unexpected openings

There is always the desire to do things in style, a way that you dreamed up by yourself or uncovered in an old history book. The stile shown below suggests romance on the moors, or meetings between neighbors. No matter what impression this structure suggests to you, it is a sensible way of vaulting a fence without discomfort. I think of the stile as a friendly tradition that deserves reinstatement. We will need that kind of neighborliness if we are soon to become stay-at-home folk.

This stile was build of heavy timbers for the strength to withstand coastal storms. The steps are so broad and the climb so little that other animals beside humans might be tempted to cross over.

In our own neighborhood there is an old house with a ragged rock wall about four feet high, and difficult to scale. But the stonemason must have had neighborly types in mind, because he included a series of double wide rocks that cantilever out from the wall as steps up one side and a matching set on the other side that go down.

We all have the urge to meander, into a neighbor's garden, or the back corners of our

own. Most of us never have room enough. Often we need to tear something out before we can plant something new. A couple of property owners at Pebble Beach worked out a good solution. Together they built a new fence, above, with two-by-four framing and bamboo screening. But they didn't run the line straight and true. Instead they notched four feet deep and eight feet wide into one property, then returned to the line for a decent interval and bayed out four feet deep and eight wide into the other. This they repeated a third and fourth time. What this gave them was new alcoves in which to grow new groupings of plants. Australian fern and big succulents fill one or two of the bays. Both families are happy with their new points of focus.

Should the conditions change, or the property owners sell out and the new owners object, the fence line can be realigned with the same timber and screening.

If a notched fence line isn't enough to keep down the wanderlust, find new openings in the vacant lot next door or down the block. Obtain permission from the owner to plant flowers and seedling trees for pleasure and for propagation. Make it a holding bed for yourself and your neighbors who might be starting a new garden. Plant perennials around the edges where they

might be allowed to remain after the lot is sold, and a vegetable garden in the center where it will receive the most sun. If vandals tend to steal your crop, solicit their help with the hoeing and weeding, and offer to share the bounty.

If there are no vacant lots around, join a community garden project and bike your way to the location. You should meet new people and find new opportunities for food and friendship.

Certain designs develop simultaneously in several cultures. Multiple lathing is one of them. There is a shadow pattern from lath structures that pleases many. In plantation gardens, summerhouses are built with two or three layers of lathing to admit light but keep out the heat of the sun. The Japanese discovered these same pleasantries for their own gardens and focused on the precision that is possible with exactly-milled strips overlaid and underlaid.

The triple-layered gate below was built by an Oriental craftsman for a California gardener. The gate is twelve feet wide and is supported on a post and lintel construction. The lintel beam is capped with copper at both ends. The gate in the center swings six feet wide, the side panels are fixed. The long diagonal strip prevents the gate from sagging. To open the gate from the outside takes a bit of doing. The lighter toned horizontal strip must be slid to a certain point before the latch can be thrown. The lath patterns change as you walk by or enter the garden. Squares of light reveal small segments of the scene beyond. The juniper shrubs in the front courtyard have been clipped according to tradition. To some Americans they appear tortured, to others they are a delight.

Entries that delight

Your entry, a door, a gate or a baffle is your first declaration of intent. It is a preliminary statement as to the nature of your garden. Its design should establish a theme and give clues as to your attitudes on gardening and garden art.

Boldness is more appropriate here than inside because you are taking a visitor from an alien environment into your own. A bit of attention-seeking may be in order.

Your entry should also give evidence of your garden's limitations. If it is not already evident, it should reveal the nature of your land—lush and green, dry and barren or subject to constant traffic just outside your garden door.

There is a certain challenge in designing an entry that does all these things well and still remains an artistic expression. Certainly it is worth the try. If no other inspirations arise, let happenstance help you. Access to an old door, a fine jardiniere or a set of ceramic tiles can prompt solutions.

If you live in the southwest where the land is bone dry, hot and mostly clay, do what the Spanish and Mexicans have done in the past to create a garden. Use the clay with straw to make an adobe mix for building blocks for a garden wall, or a house too, if you are that energetic.

Search out old mining timbers to be purchased inexpensively for use as patio beams and post and lintel construction. Assemble a gate or door of

heavy timbers bolted together with iron bolts. If growing anything is a real problem, concentrate your efforts on plants to be grown, with imported soil and humus, within the protection of the adobe walls. Southwesterners understand the struggle involved and have learned to expect good growth in the garden and a bleak facade outside. The weathered look is revered.

In the coastal areas of California the problems are fewer. Frequent fogs keep plants growing well with only occasional watering. Here a tall stand of bamboo serves as a privacy barrier along with a free-standing screen. The screen framework of two-by-fours is assembled on a flat surface and laid in a plywood form. A reinforcing wire grid is anchored to the center panel and covered with a three-inch layer of concrete. Then, while the mix is wet, many-colored pebbles are pushed in place according to a preconceived pattern. When all is dry the panel is upended and braced with heavy angle irons and long screws to the wood strips in the concrete floor. The two stones in the foreground were specially selected and set in place before the pebble-embellished paving surface was poured.

Access to this modern garden with an Oriental flavor is around the screen on the left. There are enough glimpses of the garden itself to tempt guests further. (The triple-lath gateway on a previous page is the main entrance to this Carmel garden.)

In the Old Town section of Chicago access to a rear garden on a corner lot was through a side street doorway. The garden was enclosed by a high brick wall and entered through a pair of antique interior doors from another old mansion. Old paint was removed and distinguished hardware added. The arched doors were topped with metal shields to lessen the invasion of water. Then all surfaces were sealed with a transparent coat of epoxy. The gate stands just four inches from the public sidewalk and the curb is just five feet beyond that, but the entry is inviting and the trees evident over the wall give promise of comfort.

A sideyard entry at Pebble Beach, California, shown in Color Plates 3, 12, and 22, is both practical and inventive. A skylit cubicle was constructed, between the house and the side boundary, to serve as an anteroom and small conservatory. The streetside gate is split to control seaside winds and can be closed and locked when the owners choose. The small stained-glass window appears as a beacon enticing the visitor into the inner sanctum.

The room itself is half paved, half planted with a giant fern and impatiens as ground cover. Variegated-leaf geraniums sparkle under the window. A pair of old wrought-iron gates divides the entry from the main garden.

From the rear garden the view of the cubicle and its glass ornament is still pleasant. Camellia shrubs grow below and hide a spotlight that shines on the stained glass, and bougainvilleas ramble overhead.

Our first garden was begun at the back of a downtown property with a big, old eleven-room house. By the time we signed all the papers and studied our commitments we concluded that we had little to invest in a new garden gate and fencing. We decided our garden plans would have to wait. Then we took a second look at the old chicken coop in a back corner, about eight by ten, with beautiful silver-grey unpainted boards all around. We tore it down and used the boards and the framing to build a short fence between our house and the one next door. We used galvanized nails for reconstruction and in a few days the fence looked as though it had been there as long as the house.

Still, We Needed a Gate

The gate was still a problem at the price we were willing to pay. But soon we sifted through the dust in the loft of the barn and found a broken toboggan and five old wooden skis. Our problem was solved. All of these fragments were of hardwood so it took a while to take the toboggan apart and unscrew the bindings on the skis. This accomplished, we designed a gate that needed five uprights, four spacers, and three cross boards in the widths we happened to have. Then came the fun. Each ski and each toboggan slat had to be drilled at precise points and the whole thing anchored together with screws. We had one slat left over so we put that across the front on top of the bottom cross board and just where the boys kicked the gate as they came in. We were amateurs; the gate didn't close automatically so we added a screen door spring later to bring it back in line.

We always talked of replacing the gate some day but it served us well for twenty-two years and held up better than some of our other creations. There was never a good reason for replacing it.

In time we built new side fences and shaped a garden, but that gate was a symbol of all the happiness that did happen inside that garden.

Fences . . . all kinds of designs

The fencing you add can be your first big venture, and the first perceptible difference between a backyard and a garden. You could choose shrubbery, hedging or masonry walls, but the fastest and sometimes the most effective enclosure is fencing. By this device a garden acquires limits and becomes a contained space.

As soon as the last board or picket is set, this inward-facing space is ready for use. New privacy has been achieved for your family's pleasure and well being. Distracting views have been screened, disruptive noises muffled. By setting limits on your cultivated space you have defined your zone of loving care, your play space and your studio.

Enclosed space is one of our least-expensive luxuries, a consideration never more important than today. A good fence tends to make a plot self-maintaining. Trash and dust doesn't blow in. Moisture is held in the ground longer and plants grow better in the half shade.

Fencing can be extended with inner partitions, dividing the garden further. You don't live in a one-room house, and you don't need to live in a one-room garden. Wooden fences can be clothed with climbing vines, woodbine, clematis or silver lace; concrete block or brick walls welcome English ivy, *euonymus* or *ampelopsis*. The spaces between fences can be roofed over with light trellises for further vining, and wider spans can be supported with posts at intervals.

Fences tend to concentrate many desirable circumstances. Alien wind-blown seeds are kept out, leaves and debris stay outside and harsh winds are turned away. Much of the sun's warmth can be captured and enjoyed. This newly-created microclimate can be as good for the gardener as it is for the garden.

The contained garden is a claim for privacy in a land of common ground. It matters not how it is fenced; a fence for some of us is a necessity, boldly stated. The possibilities within these spaces, although contained, remain boundless.

Most of us tend to conform because we are hesitant about expressing ourselves freely. This is a wide-spread affliction. But fortunately, for our refreshment, there are some who will always do things their own way. The photos on these pages give evidence to support this conclusion.

A fence sets the tone of a garden as does the diamond-shaped design on the following page

seen along the coast highway north of San Francisco. It also indicates its owner's craving for privacy plus a degree of concern for the pleasures of passing tourists. I also sense a bit of improvisation. The door was narrow, the boards short, and the need for a tall fence high. The woven pattern on point is a pleasing solution. While the facade is more forbidding than inviting there is hint in the ivy that is creeping under the fence that the garden beyond is lush and green.

The wattle-fenced garden (following page, below) indicates a great labor of love. It involves the gathering and smoothing of a great number of still-flexible shrub stems, five to six feet long, to be woven upward in layers between upright posts. Initially the choice was acacia, but wattling is also possible with willow or alder. The bending

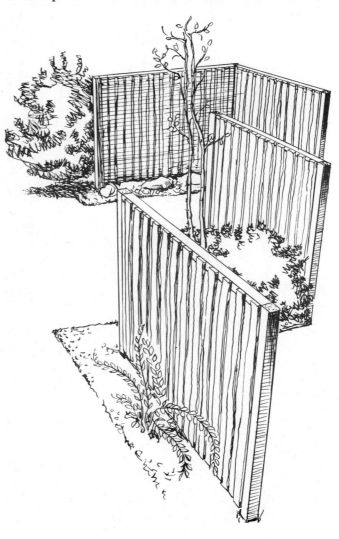

stems take skill to manage. A beginner had best start with smaller stems by making an edging for plants, as shown in the foreground.

A zealous architect from our own town produced a work of art with scrap lumber made surplus from the foundation forms of his new house. He couldn't bear to burn the boards or throw them away. He needed a partition to screen the potting bench in his wild garden, so he nailed the boards together, one on one, starting at one end and continuing with many 3-D protrusions until the lumber was used up. The fence is a shocker and a delight. It stands solid, conforming to the contours of the land, with just a little help from a pair of braces on either side of the potting bench.

Fences . . . creative solutions

I'm told that when writing a love letter, the best plan is no plan at all. Let your emotions spill out however they occur. But when building a fence, a plan is better.

Start with thumbnail sketches as a way of firming up your ideas. At this stage accurate measurements are less important. Seek instead a flow of shapes that might apply to your circumstances and your plot. Decide early whether you want the fence to be an accent feature or a transitional area. Measure your sketches against anticipated problems—hot sun that could warp boards, strong winds that might push and shove, or excessive dryness that could split or crack. Then alter your design or change materials to correct for shortcomings.

When problems are severe, start again and design directly to needed solutions.

If wind is the culprit, strengthen your fence with buttresses. Plant a second set of fence posts four feet in, to brace the new fence and serve, at the same time, as a support for a long trellis on the windward side of your plot. Hang the trellis or pergola with jasmine, honeysuckle, or if you prefer food, grape or kiwi.

If it is not in your nature to shut people out with solid fencing, settle for an open pattern with cross-hatch lathing panels running across at the four-to-six foot level. Plant rambler or climber roses to grow up and weave between the laths. This will give you relative privacy and your neighbors should not be offended. They should accept the structure as a way of growing roses for their benefit.

Whatever your design, be sure it is an artistic adjunct to your garden, not just a utilitarian necessity.

While you are boarding yourself in with a six-foot wall, preserve and enhance your own views. Design a small fern garden in the narrow space outside your bedroom window, or build a wall fountain in front of the fence where it parallels your rear terrace.

You also have the opportunity to improve your house itself. A fenced or partitioned entry court-yard can disguise awkward architectural features or simply define a more gracious approach to your front door. A courtyard fence can give you uncurtained privacy and as a result twice as much sunshine in your living room when you want it.

That same fence can screen out the glare of the late afternoon sun or, if you live on a curve, auto lights in the evening.

A good fence can help you reclaim full use of your land, space often used by neighbors as their own. It can also shape and define a parking alcove, offside, so you can claim your front yard again.

A fence of glass and wood was the best solution for this garden at Pebble Beach, in California. It modifies the winds that come off the ocean while offering a paneled glass view of the dunes and the blue sea. On days when the weather is mild the center section of the fence swings away to allow an uninterrupted view. The red maple tree in the container has been bent and curved to a graceful line with the effective but inconspicuous use of fishing weights. The entrance is an infrequently used, auxiliary access, and the redwood container is mounted on a dolly so it can be moved to one side when the gate is opened.

The work of a thoughtful gardener is evident in this transitional design between two fences of different heights. One of the fences is of narrow slats, so the transition is relatively easy to contrive. Here four slats were cut to four-and-one-half, five, five-and-one-half, and six feet to join a four-foot fence with another six feet high. Capping boards were cut to cover the lower slat and attach to the next higher one. Then, to make the joint less conspicuous the short caps were mitred where they join the inside slat. The Atherton, California, man who built this was aware of the importance of little things.

You can eliminate the need for gates if you build several fenced alcoves with narrow slot entries in-between. This Boulder, Colorado, design is based on full circles and reflects the circular motif evident in the contemporary residence.

The circular fence is double-walled for strength and finish. It covers two-thirds of a circle. Tree rounds upended in the ground complete the ring. A sunburst locust is planted on one side, a curved bench is attached to the fence on the other. Pebbles and a few larger, flat stones cover the ground and complete the design.

Fences . . . personal solutions

Today some of our finest gardens are small and personal. They are designed for their makers' selfish enjoyment and nothing more. Other gardens are intended as showplaces, real enticements that attract visitors and generate social contact. If you are gregarious, a show garden may be right for you. There is also frustration if you rely on outside praise. You may be better off with a private retreat, sustained by your own energies and for your own solace.

We may not all design quickly and well, but like Sunday painters we can learn. It is not that we wish to compete with professionals but rather reach for some of the excitement associated with art. While daring to do, we must keep our focus on our own aspirations. Let the sophisticates condemn us and our efforts as pedestrian and doomed to failure. But let's not be dissuaded. Our lives may be richer than theirs.

If eccentricity is considered to be somewhat improper, so be it. The middle of the road is a dull place. There is a lot more to see in the barrow pits to either side—wildflowers, weeds and field mice, for example—and all more intriguing than the painted yellow line in the center.

That is the Question

To fence or not to fence remains the question. For some it's a continuing debate, for others it is a firm yes or no. Few are agoraphobic, fearing open spaces, and few claustrophobic, afraid of enclosures. Today we fear nothing and everything. On one hand we campaign for wilderness preservation, on the other for private sequestered places. We insist on today's ultimate, the best of both worlds.

History tells us that gardeners have been putting up and tearing down garden walls for centuries. From the high-walled gardens of medieval castles and the herb and apothecary gardens of monasteries, man has moved toward hedged gardens and on to the broad, parterre gardens of LeNotre with their regal expanses.

Openness again became the form when Capability Brown guided the British back to the beauty to be found in uninterrupted views of the countryside. All listened but not all believed, and a good number of gardeners held to the charméd plot, the cottage garden or the formal enclosure.

American colonists brought their traditions from England. They built up fenced and orderly designs, perhaps as evidence that they could make a clearing and live gracefully in spite of the surrounding wilderness. As plantations developed across the broad land, fences were used more to contain horses and sheep than people. Through the nineteenth century attitudes toward fencing were mixed, but those who favored it

most were to be found among the lower classes with their first plot of ground. When the cities became overcrowded and people moved to the suburbs, the unbroken view and the park-like image became the goal again.

Now the suburbs are growing into large cities and the land is becoming crowded again.

People are moving into smaller houses, condominiums and townhouses. Those who hope to garden must define their courtyards with privacy walls. Some are raising up fences again, this time to regain the personal use of our private land.

It seems apparent that fences will remain a major symbol of control for gardeners. No fence goes up easily, it is sometimes offensive to neighbors, sometimes too costly. Often it must be custom-designed to solve a particular problem.

A decorative but forbidding fence line keeps strangers away from a tidewater garden in a river estuary. The wide boards were decorated with fancy tops. The gate has no handle—just mysterious holes to pull finger latches.

If you live near a school route where children linger in the afternoon, build a two-way fence with benches on either side. Children can sit and visit while you enjoy six-foot privacy on the other side. Buy standard grapestake fencing and if you don't like the dog-ear look, turn the stake upside down for a more trim finish.

If tree branches interfere with your plans for a high fence and you don't want to trim the tree, notch the upper rows of bricking sufficiently to allow the tree branches to bend in a wind.

Fences . . . Colonial designs

There is much to learn on fencing from the gardens at Colonial Williamsburg. From the simplest picket to the complex Chippendale there are scores of fine examples for review and study in the institution's one hundred display gardens. Each design is exact and can be inspiring to the owner of a traditional house. It becomes apparent immediately what good carpentry work can do for a garden.

The picket fence designs are so varied that the rare fence with a simple pointed pike comes as something of a shock. The Chippendale patterns reflect the oriental influences that were popular in England about the time that the colonists were establishing their homes in this country. These designs are complex and handsome. They do require the skill of a master craftsman or a very advanced amateur.

It seems surprising that our forefathers were able to find the time to shape pickets and fences with such style and flair. Most fence posts are hand-carved with a matching motif, consuming hours of labor.

The colonists also developed a self-closing gate that swings out if it is pushed or pulled away from the gatepost. It falls back in place between the gateposts with the help of a weight on a chain tied to an auxiliary post. This device could serve today's generation just as well, keeping the dog in or the gate closed after the children have run off to play. The picket design in the photo, left, is the spear, beautifully echoed in three-D on the gateposts.

The photos show the precision of Chippendale designs as they moved from the drawing room to the garden. The fences are designed in workshop-sized units, to be assembled on the site. The tops exactly match the posts on which they sit on the white-painted fence and show small departures in the unpainted cedar design. The hardware for hinges and latches is hand-crafted. Because of the added thickness of these designs these fences reveal a variety of light patterns with the arc of the sun.

Two fence designs meet in a back garden. The one on the left is the double pike or double sawtooth, the other the diamond cap. Other possibilities include the triple sawtooth, the inverted heart or spade design, and the onion top, shown opposite lower right. The gatepost is a mitred round of the same design. If you are looking for a winter workshop project, the carving of a series

of onion-top six-by-six posts could be an industrious venture.

Williamsburg fences make us nostalgic for the unhurried craftsmanship of long ago. When the town was first plotted, it was required that houses on the main street be at least twenty by thirty feet, and those on a back street sixteen by twenty or more. All houses were to face the street and be no more than six feet from the front property line. Fences were required by law and were to be in architectural harmony with the house. They were to be four-and-one-half to five feet high to fit the scale of the buildings they enclosed.

The plan created large rear gardens. Well-being, the experts of that time said, comes from living in an environment where the house occupies no more than one-fifth of the landscape. At Williamsburg the ratio was closer to one in seven, making it a green city. Such a relationship gener-

ates the creation of gardens, small orchards and auxiliary structures.

If you want an easier project and a lighter design, consider the triple-lath pattern made with one-half by two-and-one-half-inch strips. Set the rounded uprights on the fence frame at six-inch intervals, then run diagonal strips at a 60 degree angle on one side of the uprights and the same 60 degree angle on the opposite side of the fence. Finish each face with beaded horizontal strips, above and below, to cover the raw edges. Give the pickets a first coat of paint before you assemble the fence, and a touch-up coat after.

The sawtooth design shown in the sketch is an intriguing variation. Random-width boards are nailed in place and a template with a sawtooth pattern is used to trace the zigzag edge across the top of the fence. The sawing is done on the fence in place, letting the peaks and valleys fall where they may on the random-width boards. The boards are random, but the space between is exact—three-quarters to two inches depending upon how open a fence you want. The template may define a sawtooth that has 90 degree peaks and valleys, a conservative design, or a pattern with sharper peaks of 75 or 80 degrees, as sketched.

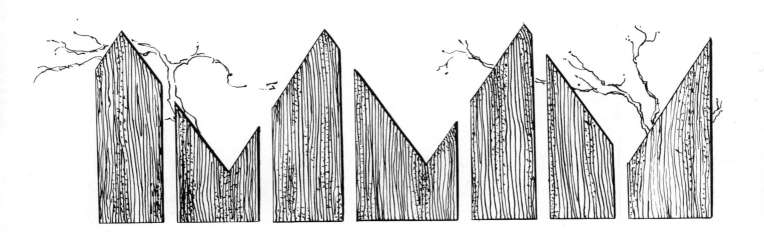

Benches . . . comfortable seats

Garden space is a fluid element. We can make it flow or interrupt it, as we choose. One of the happiest interruptions we can offer is a comfortable and inviting place to sit, a place to linger and enjoy the view, stretch your eyes or find shelter from the wind.

The rustic bench works well in its rustic setting. Cedar posts, set deep into the ground, cradle the sawed hardwood log. They also support the narrower backboard. All rough edges are smoothed with wood rasp and sanding paper and presto, if you acquired the log for nothing, you have a no-cost bench with character for permanent use. That's the way gardeners create interruptions in Virginia.

In California where the view is important, a simple, backless bench tempts guests to linger. An easy assemblage of two chimney flue concrete blocks and a broad plank does the trick. The plank is lifted away from the blocks with short boards of the same thickness as the plank to create a drop shadow line that makes the bench look stylish instead of pedestrian.

The hilltop terrace is paved with concrete pav-

ing blocks and the retaining wall mortared with a rough mix. Ivy and other vines climb the wall and a decorative tree frames the distant hills. The sculpture of a kneeling antelope is a vital and compact form, juxtaposing its sharpness and strength against the soft, rolling hills. The combination of elements from bright and precise to hazy and vague makes a visitor use his eyes for the pleasures of his senses.

If you are wanting a setup requiring no work and no care, I recommend the two words that Sam Goldwyn liked to use, *im possible*. There will always be dust that blows in, leaves that fall and surfaces that need painting, but none of these chores are oppressive. Be willing to pay a little for your privileges.

Success springs from the ability to conceive a pleasant setting in new and striking ways and to make it unique while using common materials.

When you are designing, visualize the seats you will fashion in their planned setting together with the walls or fences nearby. Be sure they live together harmoniously; if they won't, start a new plan. Most seats and benches can be moved about but if there is no other terrace elsewhere, you had better design new seats that are more in keeping.

While the garden is in work, make a sheltered place where you can think on these things or sit

and look out at your accomplishments, even on a rainy day. A couple of old kitchen chairs can do, while you and your family critics ponder these matters.

It seems apparent to me that a garden needs a sequence of spaces with appropriate furniture to tempt the user from 'room to room.' Resolution of these areas is essential if we hope to attain quality in our enclosed plot. We need always to be aware of places where land and structures meet. We must relate and interlock these elements in order to form a satisfying marriage.

There is no limit to which gardeners will go to create a comfortable sitting area. These zealous gardeners, military retirees, cut an uphill terrace at the rear of their mountainside home.

Once the terrace area was leveled with the help of heavy equipment, they proceeded to build a serpentine brick wall by dint of their own hard labor. This was a real challenge, getting the footing in, and bending the wall in scallops to conform with the site.

The wall they built would be the envy of professional bricklayers. Earthfill was then added to the back of the wall so the native ground covers could grow again. The new terrace was paved with combed concrete between redwood strips, and two antique sitzbaths were cushioned as comfortable seats. Upholstery colors are white and watermelon pink. They were inspired by two wedges of pine that a daughter made to look like slices of watermelon for a Girl Scout project. The area is small but delightful and close by their other love, a family greenhouse.

Benches . . . special seatings

We all sit down so much and so often that we have become connoisseurs. We use all the conventional devices and develop special preferences. But when someone offers us a new instrument of repose, we respond eagerly.

Who can resist sitting down with a few friends on a row of woven-reed rockers, particularly as they stand on a plantation home porch in St. Francisville, Mississippi. A chair that rocks is an unfamilar prop to the now generation. The lazy-boy seems to have taken its place. But the rocker idea is worthy and might be reinstated on any front porch. The rockers needn't match, in fact a miscellaneous collection can be more lively. But if you are interested you had better hurry because the antiquers have the word that this is a coming fad.

If you are good at making concrete castings, try starting with a couple of softwood tree trunks, and carve a set of shapely seats and stools. From these make a set of molds and cast your furniture in a weatherproof concrete. If you are skillful enough you might salvage the molds and make a second set for sister Sue. Then dig a depression in the ground where you want each piece to stand, fill it with more concrete and dimple your furniture into the oozing puddles. When all is dry and firm neither rain nor snow nor gloom of night should do them any harm.

If you don't live on the West Coast, you may have some trouble acquiring the materials for this Nepenthe bench. It is made from a thick slice of redwood with the heart missing, and is supported on stout pipes that are pounded into the ground at

precise points which match socket routings on the underside of the wood slice. The seat is about five feet in diameter and can hold a chummy group of six at one time. Because it is redwood it may be slivery but it will withstand moist weather indefinitely.

Redwood does not fare so well in dry and hot Colorado summers. It prefers to split and crack. However, if you want to try such a bench in your garden, I understand you can order a single slice of wood to be shipped in, for a fair fee. If you have access to slices of other big logs, there is no reason why the same design couldn't be used with eastern materials.

If you find yourself building many benches, you will reveal your own inclinations to rest a lot. If you don't want your laziness widely known, grow lush, stout turf and stretch out on the lawn when you are so inclined.

It is interesting to discover, in old garden prints and etchings, that gardeners in medieval times sculpted their ground to a shape similar to today's barwa chair and covered it with turf. From the old drawing, it appears to be as comfortable an arrangement as any upholstered lounge chair we use today.

Cyril Connolly boasted of his role as a lazy gardener. "Others merely live, I vegetate."

Baffles . . . privacy screens

Free-standing screens and baffles perform a valuable service for the gardener seeking privacy at low cost. A four-foot panel located at just the right place can furnish privacy to a sunbathing area, a dining table, or a reading corner. Because it is so effective, it must be used with discretion. To prevent a screen from becoming a direct affront to a particular neighbor, put it in place directly, before becoming acquainted with the individuals involved. Installed at this stage of your garden's development, it becomes an artistic device and nothing more.

Interrupt Overhead Sightlines

If you live in an area where high-rise and one-story structures are mixed, or on a hillside where others look down on your garden from above, consider installing an awning or arbor structure overhead that interferes with the line of sight of the curious.

If you are annoyed by a cluster of utility poles in the middle of your best view, add a series of columns salvaged from the razed mansion down the block and plant them in a grouping where they

can hide the unsightly while creating an attraction for yourself. If you prefer Lombardy poplars to columns, carry on. They take more patience and less muscle than the columns.

Be enterprising and inventive. See what you can make for a song. Fish kites or floating banners can ride in the breeze and give you the interference that thwarts the man with the binoculars on the balcony above. Rubber balloons can add color and obscurity for a one-day event.

Use vines on a trellis or pergola to muddle the image and give you needed shade to boot. Comes winter when the vine leaves fall away you can capture more warmth from the sun and the man on the balcony will probably be too busy to bother with sightseeing.

Incorporate screening devices in your garden plan. If your lot is narrow and one neighbor seems to be breathing down your throat, build a six-foot fence with a lath trellis above and swag it with rose climbers. Then add a series of mirrors to your side of the fence with a two-foot leave on the top of the fence to protect them from heavy rains. They can reflect the flowers in the opposite beds and make your garden seem double wide. Bring the mirrors indoors for the winter and rehang them in the spring.

If you would like to shield your front door from the one next door and you have access to a mix of short lengths of fine wood, assemble a screen of intricate design from the lumber scraps. The screen in the photo is multilayered from a 2" x 4" and 1" x 4" base, and then embellished with 1" x 3s", 2" x 2", and a great many 1" x 1" strips. A container grown *Podocarpus* adds green to the newly tiled porch stoop.

There are other reasons for screens besides privacy. They can be used to ward off chill winds or to lift air currents across a terrace and cool it in the summer. They can also shield a particular area from the heat of high noon or the sun as it sinks slowly and glaringly in the west.

Because the sun doesn't always set at the same point of the compass, a sunset screen needs to be flexible or all-encompassing. The one in the photo to the right is particularly flexible. In winter when the sun is welcomed, the screen is hooked and strapped to the inside wall of the veranda. As the days lengthen and the setting sun describes a wider arc, the louvered panels are unfolded and rolled on castors to a wider position. This way

they shade the dining table during an early evening meal while admitting a flow of air above and below the panels. The five panels, fully extended, can be latched to the column in the forward corner.

This Colorado garden is as subject to summer thunderstorms as any other; the sudden storms bring heavy rain and downspout washouts. But this thoughtful gardener has piled stone and coral in the splash block to slow the pace of the runoff. The stones also ornament an otherwide utilitarian object.

The Italian terra cotta pots hold *Sempervivums* or houseleeks. These are small rosette-shaped succulents in soft greys and white. They invite close inspection.

Uncommon retreats

Each of us need an uncommon retreat, a place to flee to when things get rough, a haven where we can unwind, heal and go forth again. It can be a simple structure, less ornate than Mr. Hearst's San Simeon, a little closer to human scale.

I have in mind a simple structure, roofed but open to garden view, or merely framed and clothed with vines, about the size of a small room. It might be a screened summerhouse in a back corner, a hexagon gazebo that can be entered from two points, with short benches in between.

The prime goals are modest comfort and a semblance of privacy—even from your family. It might be a retreat from bright sunlight or, on a porch roof, an attraction to it. It could be a triangular cabana connected to a triangular deck and both parts attached to a small dunking pool. A retreat may be without structure and no more than a table and chair on flat ground, in the shelter of an old pear tree. Retreat is a verb as well as a noun, a human instinct that might be soothed in a proper structure.

There is a hesitancy among gardeners to build a structure particularly for their own selfish use, and this is unfortunate. We plant flowers and grow trees for the same reasons but it seems less apparent to others. We seem to need an excuse, not a reason, for building.

A reading platform is such a legitimate excuse there should already be one in every backyard, but there isn't. It's a fine idea and takes so little construction to accomplish. This excellent design in Lisle, Illinois, includes a wood platform to allow for year-round use, two eight by eight inch timbers as uprights, and a ladder-like roof of two-by-fours held together with wood doweling. Weatherproof furniture with weatherproof cushions encourages continued use. Vines climb both posts, and herbs grow in beds and containers round about. A series of small tiles commemorating the horticultural talents of Linnaeus, Michaux, Redouté and Le Nôtre decorate the stone wall. A similar grouping might be constructed beside a wooden fence.

The grand swimming pool at San Simeon and the stairways and terraces that overlook it give evidence of the opulence of the once-vital fairytale world of William Randolph Hearst. Meticulously-clipped cypress and live oak clothe the ornate Hollywoodian architecture, while marble statuary oversee the patterned water. It's impressive but hardly the retreat you would expect on the top of a mountain.

A streetside driveway and garage were reclaimed for family use. A high fence was built along the front property line and stonewalled beds were superimposed on the driveway concrete. A large piñon tree was added on the left and the parkway elm became a borrowed view. The concrete behind the stone walls was punctured before garden loam was added to the beds to assure easy drainage. The two-car garage, behind the camera, became a comfortable family room with a window view of the new terrace.

Gazebos and lath houses

With our added leisure we should find time for the construction of gazebos and lath houses to bring pleasure to these liberated hours. It is just a short flight of fancy from humdrum chores to delightful assignments, but you need to do your own assigning. And don't tell me you haven't the time. We are never, not ever, as hard-pressed as our forefathers and they found the time. I'd like to think we have an obligation to our horticultural past to continue with their niceties. How long has it been since you have seen a fountain or water shoot, a private pavilion, a labyrinth or a mosaic paving? It is not that we care less but that we are going so fast we miss the whimsies. Are we forgetting the restorative effects of follies and fancies? Arbors, pergolas and trellised walks are the exception instead of the rule in our times. Sundials and statues, by tradition, should be as much a part of our gardens as the fireplace, sunny window and handsome entry are a part of our homes.

Of course I know that there are lovely lath structures hidden away in private gardens across the country. That is why they are so difficult to find. Mail order houses offer patterns for ornate Victorian beauties that would challenge the skills of the most expert amateurs. I know rustic summerhouses exist and conventional gazebos are installed. It is just that I would like to see many more of them, or at least know that they are proliferating.

Sometimes whimsy lifts its head very high, as in this fanciful tubular gazebo by Denver artist Robert Anderman. Little more than an L-shaped bench in a garden meadow, it becomes a destination for garden visitors and a retreat for family members. The fact that the sculpture is utilitarian does not subtract from its artistic message. There is the pleasure of being sheltered within, and the mystery of wondering, within what? There is a bit of a giraffe lurking 'within' for me. I would guess that you might see something else. If a De Kooning painting of a woman looks like a boy on a bicycle learning to swim, why can't a gazebo look like a giraffe?

It is possible as we grow up that we become reluctant to admit to playfulness. I get that notion when I take guests through our own garden. They look puzzled when I show them the 'Livingston Seagull' our younger son made from chrome car bumpers. It has a four-foot wingspread and hangs by thin wires from the top of the back fence. The same puzzlement is evident when I point out husband Guy's stove leg Modigliani mounted on a pipe standing in the lilac bushes. My own discovery, the dancing torso, elicits no comments at all. I gather we are on the wild side of the playfulness scale.

A California gardener with a more conservative approach solved two garden problems with twin lath parasols. She brought partial shade to the tuberous begonias growing in the raised beds beneath and created an obstruction of gentle beauty that interfered with her neighbor's view of her rear deck. In a short time the wisteria vines on the center poles climbed into the superstructure to create a dramatic floral display. Camellias mingle with the begonias to assure a succession of bloom.

But take note of the taste and caring evident in the parasol design. The wood used is of first quality and the laths are neatly mitred to the hip 'roof'. The parasols are of slightly different height and the left hand unit about one foot farther away from the fence. The structures are light and airy in appearance, not an oppressive barrier to the neighbor. The six-foot fence behind the lath parasols is of good design and makes use of six-inch boards placed at three-foot intervals and

covered on the reverse side with like boards and at the same spacing. That means that the design is just as good on the neighbor's side as on the owner's.

This is a consideration with fencing that we seldom make. Most of us figure that if we pay for the fence we are privileged to look at the 'good' side and the neighbor is lucky to see the framework and the knotty side of the boards. Does this mean we have a double standard in gardening too?

Dare I suggest that we be aware of the consequences of all we do in our gardens, whether it is the positioning of a tree in the southeast corner of our property or the erection of a tree house on our north boundary where its shade may interfere with the growth of our neighbor's vegetable garden. If the tree in the southeast corner is a locust or a catalpa, the leaves, the twigs and the pods will all blow onto your neighbor's property when the first northwesterlies ride in.

Other retreats

The craving for a tree house is widespread and exists among people of all ages. It come from the desire to be above others, in a wind-swept place that also moves with the wind.

If you don't have a tree large enough to support such a structure, do what these high-country Coloradoans did. Build a house between the trees. Build it high enough to be up in the flexible parts of the tree trunks so every part bends in the wind in unison. Lay a platform between two stout tree poles which have been lashed to the live uprights. Then add your lightweight side walls, a door and window, and put a roof of corrugated metal up top. If you want more light, do the roof with corrugated plastic instead.

Getting back on the ground, there seems to be something psychological about man's need for protection against the sky. If we had been living in caves I would say that we found the light too bright, or the brunt of the storms too severe. Then there is the cold and the feeling we'll never get warm without a roof over our heads. But in a garden the biggest problem is the heat of the sun. Gardeners wear broad-brimmed hats and lady visitors carry parasols. There is always the desire to get out of the sun and into the shade.

When there is no shade, we make shade. On a barren site it is possible to build an attractive shelter with wood beams and a considerable

number of yards of awning material. This terrace uses pairs of 2 by 10 inch beams supported on 4 by 4 inch posts. The awning material is threaded between the beams and stretched just enough to hold its shape, not so tight that it shrinks and tears in the first rainstorm. The cloth is folded under at each end for more secure tacking. Its bright color and lively shade pattern adds vitality to the patio. Bright red ladder-back chairs match the candy-striped awning and annual seedlings, rocket snaps, are started in half-barrel tubs. The fence, at five feet, hides much of the barren land beyond.

If the canvas is of good enough quality, it can be taken down in the fall and returned to the scaffolding in the late spring. The terrace in mid-winter will be more useful if the sun comes in unimpeded. Because the awning structure was added after the concrete terrace had been laid, the floor between the posts was finished with a concrete base and ceramic tiles over.

Friends who own a local nursery that used to be out on the edge of town and now stands in the middle on a main circle route are master improvisors. When the power line along their route was converted to high-tower transmission, the utility pole crossbars were available in eight-foot lengths for the taking. They gathered the wood and insulators from nearby poles and built an octagon structure with P.U.C. framing and secondhand glass. To this they added a plastic roof. The work in progress looked so good to them that they enrolled in evening classes in stained-glass making and created a series of pieces to decorate their glass house. Now it is more than a summerhouse; with most of the windows and door closed, it is also a retreat on a warm winter day.

The remaining timbers were combined with other salvaged wood to make a grid privacy screen between their home and their nursery center. To this they added their collection of green and blue glass insulators, including the ones newly-acquired, to fill the grid spaces.

These people pursue gardening with a vigor. They grow giant pumpkins and save the largest to dry slowly and stand as a brilliant ornament on their dining terrace the following year or until they can produce a pumpkin that is larger still.

This is the same man who, when he gave up bowling, brought his ball out into the garden to stand on top of a fence post as a durable work of art. His wife raises cacti of extraordinary beauty in pots, outdoors in the summer and indoors in winter. The tougher varieties winter over in the new glasshouse. Both enjoy their do-it-yourself pleasures. They believe that keeping active is the best relaxation there is.

Other traditions

We need to nurture the instinct to enrich our lives and our gardens. We need to remain alert to the opportunities that come into view—the well-turned finial, the nicely-proportioned bench and the thoughtfully-appointed potting shed.

The features and follies we create will be only as good as the printed plans dictate, or our tastes make them. Personal preferences and inclinations build up slowly and discernment for what is appropriate follows.

Always we should pursue the careful arts of assembly and construction but we need reasons for doing so. There should be the sound of hummingbirds sizzling through, and hint of bells and water. There is no point to sitting in a handsome gazebo if there is nothing round about to titillate the senses. Further we need time for quiet reflection, places to experience the most important sense we have—the sense of wonder.
The designs we create make islands of order. They are most appreciated by the mind's eye.

This well-crafted bench is simple in design with curving, graceful lines. The bench is painted to a deep green to serve as a natural companion for the neighboring *Magnolia grandiflora* tree. It too glistens in the rain and its leaves curve into ovals. At once we recognize the rightness of this accessory and concede to the impulse to linger in the sheen even though it is raining.

If you have a small stream or arroyo and a cabinetmakers's skill, build a bridge-bench in careful detail. And when it is finished and installed, sit upon it and listen to the sound of the stream as it passes beneath and to the warble of birds as they communicate in the woods. Prune the trees to arc overhead but then look around at the leaf patterns, not the skill of your sawing.

Become aware of materials and how they can work for you. For a formal setting with a great many trees and blossoms, make or select a strap-iron sette that will be comfortable to sit upon and inviting. It will be more than decorative; it will be self-cleaning. Azalea blossoms and tree leaves will not gather on the seat. The winds will carry them away quickly. When the rains come it will dry off in short order and it will be dry underfoot because of the extra brick platform.

If you are doing an arbor, choose the best material for your climate and the style of your garden. Determine the kind of vines you wish to use before finalizing the design. Some vines clothe a framework tightly, others drape themselves in wide festoons and need to be tied in place. A trumpet creeper, *Campsis,* under 'ideal' conditions can run rampant, climb a nearby roof and thread its way under the shingles. Silver Lace, *Polygonum auberti,* climbs twenty-five feet high if it has a chance or builds up into a matte so thick the lower stems die to form further support.

Vines follow their own whims in their own way. If encouraged to grow they just vegetate. Then when they see that you are giving up, they strike out in all directions and at double time.

If you wish to outfit your garden without building structures, try narrowing your activities to furniture. Place an old oak table and matching chairs at the far end of the garden to extend your range and encourage fuller use of the plot.

Or bring in rocks for a fireplace base in a wide clearing and then add eighteen-inch cuttings of tree rounds to serve as stools around your fire. If the idea works for you, you might dig a pit for the hearth and use the soil you dig out to shape an earth-circle of 'chair backs' for your visitors to lean against.

If you fall heir to a summerhouse or gazebo that seems skimpy to you, remove one or two side railings for easier access and then enlarge the structure's dimensions with a circular terrace, five feet wide around all sides. Pave it with bricks or tree slices, or cover it with marl for easy compaction. Then add a few more benches around the new perimeter to bring the facility to the size you prefer.

Tie your new structures to your house in some harmonious way. Build the foundation wall of the same concrete or stone used on the house. Embellish or pave the surfaces with the same kind of brick and color as used elsewhere, and cover your new structure with a roof of like pitch. Paint or stain the new material to the same colors as used on the house trim. Introduce some of the same detailing and landscaping at your front entry as is incorporated in your latest project. Strive for harmony all along the way and the new structures will soon look as though they were built at the same time as the house.

The fact that nothing then looks brand new does not lessen the value of your various appointments. If anything it indicates that they were all a unified part of the original grand scheme.

Structures for easier care

Low maintenance and easier care obviously give you more time to *enjoy* your garden. If this were practiced more often people wouldn't speak of going outside to *work* in the garden. Gardening is no more *work* than playing a piano or shaping a sculpture. All three activities take thought and muscle, but somewhere along the line gardening picked up a bad name.

This may be because early gardens were a homeowner's only entertainment and half of his family's subsistence. That puts horticulture in a life-and-death class and away from art and music. That does seem a shame, it is so pleasureful as well.

To change this image, gardeners need to build a sense of permanence in their new structures. They need to use durable materials, stone, concrete, and weather-resistant woods. When salvaged material is used it should be durable also.

Of course there can be place for a beautiful basket that won't last more than one or two seasons, a brightly-colored canvas or fabric that will fade in a few months, but concentrate on the easing of duties and chores that need to be done over and over again. Choose furniture that is weather-resistant and does not have to be moved in and out. Select paving materials that can be hosed down rather than swept. If you have a lawn, shape it to a shallow dish form to reduce watering chores and to make the mowing easier than with a rectangular shape that requires you to lift and turn the mower at each corner five or six times around. In a single season with twenty or more mowings, that counts up to a lot of extra pushing and tugging on a big machine. Then while you are cutting down on labor, add a mowing strip around the lawn, of brick or concrete, to eliminate all hand-trimming.

gether as a sturdy support. The weight of the slab is sufficient to hold itself in place. Rains may come and leaves may blow, but the unit it self-cleaning and always ready for use. Marble slabs are still to be found in wrecking yards as remnants from old buildings with marble bank counters or fancy washrooms.

If building a railing around a deck is too big a project, build a three-holer bench instead. Anchor it to the edge of the deck and fill the holes with pots of geraniums or other plants in season.

If you are dealing with desert sun, build a ramada with a few tree limbs and a load of palm fronds. Then design furniture of concrete, as in this Tucson garden, and pebble the ground and mortar the pebbles with cement. Care will be minimal and the patio an oasis of shade by day and a real delight by night.

To make planting and hoeing easier, build raised beds with enough of a top shelf to give you a choice of stooping or sitting. Mulch your plants with humus to lessen the need for cultivation, humus that can be turned into the soil in the fall for enrichment. Start small caches of compost under shrubs and trees to benefit woody growth and to have it convenient for scooping up when you need to nourish a particular plant nearby. Grow perennials for pleasure year after year, with little care, and annuals to brighten a dull corner or bolster your perennial display.

Think twice before you make any additions to your garden plan. Think of the potential *work* involved as well as the likely leasure. Protect yourself from hardships and you will enjoy more.

Build an all-season garden table using a marble slab and three smooth concrete blocks wired to-

CHAPTER FOUR

Embellishments

Gardening is really a labor of love—a love of sheltering trees, delightful flowers, thick turf and all the comforts these things bring to our lives. There is fascination with spurting growth, twining stems, sudden bloom and miracle seed. Our gardens grow in modest and significant ways but who is to say which is important?

We routinely aim for good design, appropriate plant materials and easier care. Beyond this we have the desire to embellish and enliven. We are pleased with ourselves when the bright blue lobelia grows among the Dainty Bess roses, or the clump of tall-bearded iris, Lilac Festival, welcomes the old-fashioned lemon lilies, *Hemerocallis flava,* and the sweet-smelling rocket, *Hesperis.* These little details may not tell much of the scope of our gardens but it gives evidence of our drive and discernment.

Feel More Alive

From here it doesn't take much to tempt us from standard challenges to the more intriguing opportunities to be found in features and ornaments. These excursions generate a creative force that makes us feel more alive, and contributes to our sense of well-being.

One man I knew said, "If I am to have only one life to live, let me live it as a gardener." This sounds a bit dramatic, but while seldom voiced, it is the aim of many of us. Gardening mellows our days and nourishes our sense of anticipation. When I compare gardening to other activities, nothing but the growth and maturing of our children is so rewarding.

A bookseller friend of ours finds other compensations. "I'm with people all day long—gardening is a nice change. Sometimes I think I should have been a professional lighthouse tender." His entry

garden of native and apt plants is open to neighborhood view, but the rear half-acre is designed for his own and his family's pleasure. A string hammock hung between oaks in a small ravine makes a fine reader's corner. A cabaña alcove beside the pool has become the gathering point for a collection of oddments that have sentimental value. An old mirror reflects the ocean-like view of the Kansas plains; skulls of horse, cow and goat add an eerie beauty. A small sailboat begs to be taken into the pool and a volleyball and Frisbee await the challenges of more athletic types. Over all is a giant thermometer offering constant advice on the ambient temperature.

Tender Loving Care

The carpentry work of this bookseller/craftsman is both practical and far out. All exposed timbers have been smoothed and rounded with tender loving care for sliver-safety and for the pride to be found in a fine edge or a well-turned corner. The home-built cabaña is oriented to the east to catch the first warmth of morning and is 'barely' visible to near neighbors. Just thirty steps from the house, the area is off-limits to daily intrusions. With such stipulations the lot is big enough to hide away in. With its various appointments and embellishments it is a grand place for summer escapism, a charming retreat for fun, sun and spiritual refreshment.

Another man of my acquaintance spent his retirement years in his garden. He grew fine orchard fruit and superb vegetables, but he found other pleasures in making garden adornments. His style was primitive but quite delightful. He enjoyed wood carving and especially the carving of small animals. He spent winter days shaping

excitement that elevates the pink-on-pink scene to new heights.

A California gardener, originally from Colorado, found great joy in the subtropical blooms in her new garden. She could hardly bear to discard begonia and camellia blooms as they began to fade. She discovered that she could sustain them for a few extra days by clipping the full-blown blooms and laying them in a large copper dish near a small fountain, together with ivy cuttings she could not resist propagating. To this she added several small glass floats. With her continued care, the floral arrangement was self-perpetuating and a pleasant feature in the garden.

The Value of Focus

Many gardeners recognize the value of a statue of St. Francis and the birds as a focus on a terrace. The flowers are no prettier, the birds no more plentiful, but there is a place to rest one's eye and then look out again. St. Francis ornaments come in all sizes and styles. This beholder of nature may be cast in bronze, life-size, or shown in a miniature wooden shrine on a stone wall. In recent years the craftsmen of Santa Fe have been gathering cottonwood tree trunks from New Mexico river bottoms and shaping the soft, white wood into religious figures. St. Francis is a favorite subject among these craftsmen.

In today's gardens, more often than not, it is the features that are remembered. Ornaments and embellishments can add to a gardener's pleasures. This chapter considers these enticements and suggests to you an exploration of this often frivolous preoccupation.

Color—A Fine Tool

Embellishments can be floricultural as well as ornamental, as the color photo of potted hydrangeas will attest. Such a display takes some planning and a back-corner sun pocket where you can cultivate other flowering plants, in pots, as replacement displays. Grow a half-dozen potted geraniums and bring them into your entry for use when the potted tulips have faded. Cultivate tuberous or fibrous begonias, marguerites or cinerarias, whatever you are able to grow outside your front door. Marigolds, petunias and zinnias can make fine late summer shows. All this takes good potting soil and a lot of pots to support the rotation process, but the displays can be showstoppers in almost every season.

and painting small birds to be mounted on fence posts. He had a whole family of small skunks that romped in the sedum. He apparently grew weary of trimming grasses from under his fences so he laid ribbons of concrete under each fence to eliminate the chore. He died the past year after a full life and he left a fanciful garden.

A close friend is an exquisite gardener. She works primarily with a pastel palette and produces garden displays of great beauty. In the spring she presents pink crystal tulips in a bed of bleeding heart *Dicentra spectabilis* under a rose-pink Hopa crab apple tree that is encircled with brick paving. *Viburnum Carlesii* shrubs that bloom beside the house in pale pink have a fine fragrance. The area is indeed a spring bower but all is not focused on sweetness and light. The terrace sette, lounge and dining chairs have seat covers upholstered with brilliant fabric designed by her daughter, a professional artist. The bright cerise and purple hues introduce an element of

Embellishments from the past

Garden art has many facets and offers as many opportunities, but for us it is really just a matter of doing the right thing in the right space. If you feel comfortable with the past, make use of symbols from earlier times to show your affections. Give a precious relic a place of honor in your garden. Years ago, while visiting a James River garden, I discovered an oriental statue of luminous white marble standing in a dark, wooden box just inches larger than itself. The garden was overcrowded with big trees and dark and dank from heavy shade, but the old statue of a Chinese maiden, in her weathered shelter, captured my attention and my heart. She stood at a slight tilt, but in a place she must have stood for a century. The magic of the moment still lingers.

The ancient Mayan stool is a pre-Columbian chair, and an archeological find. Placed in front of a broad wooden column, it suggests an earlier use, perhaps as the throne it may have been.

The unusual garden ornament on page 92 may not be easily identifiable. It is a fragment of stone, a corner spire from a church steeple. It was transported, perhaps as a gift to Thomas Jefferson, from Oxford, England, to stand among pines in a garden in Charlottesville, Virginia.

Few of us have access to such prestigious relics but we do have opportunities to acquire local

mementos. In our own garden we have a large, white-glazed, terra cotta tile of a fleur-de-lis. It is from the facade of a turn-of-the century theatre on Pikes Peak Avenue. After much travail, the fine old and still useful building was torn down to make room for a parking lot. We call our tile a tombstone to a lost cause.

Collect for Personal Use

The collection of off-beat items is open to everyone. In addition to having personal worth, an item with historical significance might increase in value in close correlation with other collectibles. The value of these objects follows the rise and fall of the stock market. It seems better to focus pursuit on personal usefulness than to bank on future profits.

The world of antiquers is filled with venturesome and sentimental people who treasure remnants from the past. At first I was surprised to discover that many who collect antiques are also gardeners. This may be a natural consequence. When collectors exhaust the show space and storerooms within their homes, it is right that they turn to their gardens. Here they can display distressed or weatherproof items to good advantage. These look good in the company of bright flowers, and equally appropriate in the dust and dirt of winter or the fallen leaves and faded flowers of fall. An item that appears rough and worn in a pristine interior may seem to be in prime condition in a garden. Furthermore, many an-

tiques were designed for outdoor use and look far better in a garden nook than a living room alcove.

Make Your Own

If you can't find what you want or afford what you find, make your own ornaments. Carve a large figurehead from a tree trunk, for your imaginary ship.

Do a cigar store Indian from another chunk of wood. Copy patterns to be found in books on American antiques or create your own designs based on your own recollections as gleaned from TV westerns or other sources. Paint the carved Indian in extraordinary colors and then rub and scuff the surfaces to give the piece a distressed look, similar to the nicks and bruises the carving might have acquired while standing for a hundred years on Main Street.

If that seems to be more years than you wish to retrace, consider salvaging a more recent wooden propeller to hang between your high trees. There it can hang idle or fly once more as it catches the wind.

The beginning of a garden can seem awesome if you are new to gardening. There are so many decisions to be made on design, plant materials and structures either simultaneously or in rapid succession. Even though you plan to build in easy stages over a period of several years the need for decisions begins at once, and attitudes must be established early. I hope ornamentation is part of your plan.

Fig. 1. Good structural design enhances this Carmel Point garden. The half door offers privacy to the inner garden room when desired. *(Pages 54 and 59)*

Fig. 2. Colorado's Gambel oaks encircle a Zen garden added to a native site. Ground covers and white stone edge a simple rock grouping. *(Pages 50, 101 and 168)*

Fig. 3. A skylit cubicle serves as a garden entry and sub-tropical room. Australian fern, impatiens and geraniums complement the stained-glass ornament. *(Pages 64 and 160)*

Fig. 4. A seacoast garden with Aralia, juniper, Australian flax and Monterey pine is brightened by a Japanese parasol and cushioned reed chairs.

Fig. 6. An old tree stump became an asset in a garden with a split-level cut that reveals decorative heartwood and supports a figurine. *(Pages 101 and 140)*

Fig. 5. Water warms in the sun in a cast-iron tub that finds new use in a fenced bedroom garden. By afternoon the water is tepid and tempting. *(Page 176)*

Fig. 7. Spring is a celebration in this Colorado garden. Flowering almond shrubs and a red-veined crab set the tone; tulip and daffs follow. *(Page 166)*

Fig. 8. Blue lobelia edges a pink flagstone path to a blue entry door. A well-pruned Russian olive tree offers a comforting feeling of shelter. *(Pages 50 and 162)*

Fig. 9. A bold planting of calendulas and ice plant upstage the raw ground in Palo Verde, California. Rocks and Dusty Miller get second billing. (Page 160)

Fig. 10. A figure modeled from auto repair putty by Meg Anderson gives focus to a planting of miniature iris and sweet rocket in a June garden. *(Page 162)*

Fig. 11. A merry-go-round has-been becomes a fine accent beside a brick-walled perennial bed of day lilies, phlox and anchusa. *(Page 109)*

Fig. 12. A Barbara Karst bougainvillea festoons a garden room and complements the stained-glass-window light of vining morning glories. *(Pages 64, 124 and 160)*

Fig. 13. A collection of prickly cacti summer on a picnic table. Together, they have more impact than a scattering of individual plants. *(Pages 50, 168 and 177)*

Fig. 14. Colors mingle and clash in this flamboyant garden of roses, annuals and perennials. A petunia tree stands at center stage. *(Page 164)*

Fig. 15. Succulents *Crassula argentea, Kalanchoe tomentosa,* and *Agave mitriformis* grow in big pots beside an adobe tree well bench. *(Pages 18 and 168)*

Antiques and unusuals

If you aspire to antiquing but have not had experience in this art, let me suggest a few ways to address the market. The size of your pocketbook is less important than your sense of taste. Your appreciation of the whimsical and the incongruous can also be useful. You will still need a handful of money in dimes or dollars, depending upon the market, to deal with the seller on an instant basis.

As a beginning, turn to the 'A's in the Yellow Pages as an early reference point. From the information listed there, you should be able to locate local antique shops, art galleries, art schools and auction houses. Then set out to become acquainted with these opportunities. Your first few visits should be as a listener and a looker. Do not allow yourself to be fast-talked into a purchase. With antique prices where they are, dealers are accustomed to the hesitant buyer. Most of them realize that a soft sell is best. It may be fun to be daringly extravagant, but it is smarter to be wise. Most auction houses encourage their customers to visit their showrooms on the days preceding the sale, and will accept bids on prescribed items. This service has several advantages. It allows you

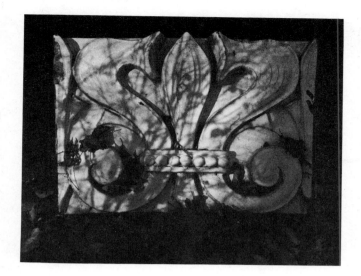

to shop at your leisure on non-auction days and prevents you from being carried away by your enthusiasms in the heat of competitive bidding on the day of the sale. When you leave your maximum figure on a fixed bid with the clerk, you may still be able to get the object for less. This occurs on the day of the sale when no one else bids aggressively.

In art galleries you may be able to get a bargain if business is slow, particularly near the end of the month. You may be able to barter with students in art schools who are willing to trade a small sculpture for photographs of drawings in their portfolios, or for houseplants to dress up their dormitory room.

Involved in all these pursuits is constant evaluation. There is always the possibility that you will goof. But this isn't critical. If you make a mistake, you learn fast. Once you recognize it and correct it you can move on to other mistaken opportunities.

To be a scrounger, you must also be flexible. If, for instance, you find a wrought iron gay-nineties fence available for a song, pause long enough to determine whether it would conflict with materials you are already using. However, if you value the fence above all others, be ready to discard that bamboo partition you are already using, and trade in the polished aluminum chairs for something more in keeping.

The strange head is nothing more than an iron stove leg which we found on our mountain land in a nineteenth-century midden heap. Guy claimed

it immediately and named it a Modigliani, after the French painter of tall, slender portraits of women. To press the connection further he added the almond-shaped eyes and small mouth. Now the piece is mounted at eye level on a slender black pipe. It is a pleasant surprise to find among the lilac bushes.

The antique wooden wheelbarrow is hand-crafted and loaded with style. It is difficult to find tools as handsome as this made by modern tool manufacturers. It blends nicely with its environment. Today's tools are either fireman-red or kelly-green with chrome trim, whether they are carts or lawn mowers.

An artist friend of ours threatened to launch a new garden tool line, using military camouflage patterns to surface his wheelbarrows and carts. His selling point was the ability of such equipment to blend so well with the scene that you would not have to put them away when not in use.

My own solution is to paint each new garden tool with a coat of the same grey-green paint we used on our house. In addition to the harmony this engenders, the tools seldom stray far from home. Our trash cans got the same treatment. If they are lost, they are quickly returned. Further, the cans fade into the scenery a lot better than when they were a shiny galvanized metal.

I wonder too about plastic garden hose. Do the manufacturers really think that grass is that brilliant a green? Perhaps what we need is a campaign against incongruities as much as one for embellishments. I wonder about milkboxes that carry the name of the dairy in red, white and blue lettering. I painted ours after some twenty years of tolerance and the milkman took it away and gave me a new one. I protested and he brought it back but couldn't understand my reasoning. I wonder too about chain link and grapestake fences that are commercially installed and carry a metal nameplate carrying the company's imprint. For the price fences bring today, we shouldn't have to carry advertisements forever after.

But I stray from my original goal. I ask you to give antiques and unusuals a chance. Remember that one man's discard is another man's treasure. If you see something in a friend's cellar or attic that strikes your fancy, be elaborate in your praise. If he or she says, ''That was my great uncle's, and I prize it above all others,'' back away. But if the reply is, ''That old thing? I'd like to get rid of it,'' you've got it made. You win some and lose some, but it is nice to be nice anyway.

With each small acquisition both you and your garden will blossom. Call it enrichment. All this takes a bit of reaching, but in addition to the visible rewards there should also be new insights into your own personality quirks and hidden talents.

The designs we create or assemble are often the illogical expression of our own subconscious. But such exercises are useful if only to reveal our creative potential. The effort, if it does nothing else, can trigger a sense of release for the spirit.

Jade trees acquire new importance when displayed in containers that have greater value. Here blue-glazed pots from China introduce a new elegance to an otherwise common houseplant. And these impressions pyramid. Because the plants look so good in their 'new' containers, the gardener feels compelled to give them extra care and more careful pruning, and evidence of that caring generates further care.

Small refinements

Our gardens today are intended to be sensitive and personal. They need to be geared to our self-ish pleasures, and designed for our own solace. When we grow weary of making big decisions, we can retreat to detailing and small refinements and poke along as we choose.

Living as we are in an era when most of us have new leisure time, a little surplus income, and freedom from drudgery, we feel liberated and able to fashion our own creations. Suddenly we can live as aristocrats have lived for centuries, doing what we choose to enliven our lives, polish our skills and elevate our talents.

If you wish to proceed slowly, consider turning for a while to garden detailing. Even if you make a mistake as you design, your missteps will be a small matter because the designs will still be dominated by your intention.

Even as you work, whether you are making a utilitarian sunshade, a windbreak or a drainage ditch, inject small refinements in your work. Design the sunshade to be lightweight and of slim line. Think of the strength of the thin sticks that frame a bamboo parasol and design accordingly. When you build a windbreak, consider adding side wings that can be both decorative and useful. Buttressing can strengthen the structure and inject cross shadows to add minutiae to the broad expanse.

If you are obliged to define a drainage path across your property, gather the rocks that lay on the surface and group them on either side of the streambed, into clusters to support a few rock-garden plants. Then surface the ditch casually with a mosaic of multi-colored pebbles and stones. If you have boulders available, roll in and anchor a few where they might interrupt and alter the headlong flow. Add puddle plantings of native ground covers to soften the edges and make the ditch look like a preference rather than a necessity. Refine as you go—always.

Design Thoughtfully

Since your garden may be the most important artistic effort you make in your life, do it thoughtfully and well. Take note of the footscraper you have beside your door. It may not be as graceful as this design by an earlier craftsman, but it can be equally appropriate.

A young man in industrial construction brought home a slice of an eight-inch I-beam. The slice was no more than four inches thick, but the piece, laid down on its burred edge, made a perfect footscraper at no cost, graceful in its proportions as a skyscraper is graceful.

It is so easy for us to say we haven't the time for these grace-notes. We are busy and have many other demands on our leisure hours—tennis, golf, back-packing. But we still have more free time than our forefathers, plus a lot of short-cuts and inventions that make life easier. It is a matter of wanting. We could shape a fine footscraper or cap a special fence post. How can I make these things seem important? We still take pains to see that our automobile is fine-tuned, that our skis are waxed just so or our hair is trimmed to the right degree between groomed and casual. Why not the garden detail?

Others Find Time

The brass-topped bridge post is in St. Louis at the Missouri Botanical Gardens, but it was made by artisans from Japan. It is one of several bridge posts in the Japanese Garden there and exemplifies the refinements pursued by others. The making of a *giboshi* is a much-revered garden art.

The British, who live life closer to our own tempo, build beehives with Chippendale domes

Color Illustrations

In the front color section are two illustrations of thoughtful refinements and tasteful embellishments. The first, Color Plate 2, is the garden of a retired couple in Colorado Springs. They have spent a lifetime shaping a six-acre plot in the foothills. The husband is the family horticulturist and the wife the garden's designer. Spry and still young after fifty-eight years of gardening together, they remain in charge of their garden projects.

Through the years they have used the natural gifts of the land well, taking daily pleasure in their boulder-strewn landscape with a native cover of scrub oak, *Quercus ilicifolia,* Colorado blue spruce, *Picea pungens,* and soaring pine, *Pinus pondorosa.*

On their travels they became interested in the merits of oriental theories, and reshaped some of the areas accordingly. Entry is up a winding road where the native cover is embellished with wild currant, decorative grasses and mountain ground covers.

Here they developed the Japanese concept of Zen gardening. In the center of the rough Colorado land they created a cared-for place. They arranged the stones for gentle contemplation and circled them with low-growing plants native to the region. They defined the area with light-colored pebbles and were content with their effort and the peace their Zen garden offered. They pruned nearby oaks carefully to emphasize their strong lines and shaped neighboring trees somewhat less so that all blended well together.

The other color photo, Color Plate 6, illustrates a smaller project at Pebble Beach, California. It shows an ingenious way to 'refine' a tree stump. The owners cut away a portion of the ungainly stump, down the center and at a right angle, to one side, near ground level. The cutting reveals the beauty of the heartwood and the shape became a kind of throne for the oriental figurine it now supports. By this manipulation, an eyesore became a refinement of considerable merit.

because they find the basic beehive very dull. They preserve and hollow out giant dead trees in place to make playhouses for their children. Access is through a small door, hardly large enough to allow the gardener in to hollow out the tree in the first place.

Traditionalists among them save every architectural fragment that comes their way. What they cannot use in some practical manner they arrange in a shady corner as old ruins, where they will become covered with emerald green moss to make them doubly intriguing.

There are detailers in our country, but not nearly enough of them. A very energetic woman in our city gardens on the edge of a mesa. The site is steep and south-facing. Over a period of some twenty years she has developed a tapestry of extraordinary beauty, primarily with ground-hugging plants that can withstand the brunt of the Chinook winds. The soil was never good and the rocks were many, but she has rearranged her materials to good advantage, cushioning the land with robust succulents nestled in pockets of richer soil. She has used the rocks to make stepping terraces that allow visitors to negotiate the steep slope, down on one side and up on the other. She herself gambols up and down, tending each plant as an individual on her one-acre site.

Sundials

"Life is really boring," says country music singer, Kenny Rogers. "You have to throw a kink in there somewhere." If this is true, why not try a sundial in your garden, and avoid boredom. This strange, silent instrument is all charm and mystery. By its own devices it charts the imperceptible flight of the sun across the sky and it does this without the intrusion of ticking noises or the sounding of bells.

A Pagan Device

The dial stone appeals to our pagan instincts to worship the sun. And rightly so, for what gardener is not a sunworshipper? The instrument is steeped in fanciful history. Its mysteries date back to the days of ancient Chaldea in the Persian Gulf.

A dial charts the time with the edge of a shadow cast, by the sun, unto a metal gnomon, angled at 45 degrees. Most dials are round, a few rectangular, and mark the hours with Roman numerals. Installation must be in a place of full sunshine, on a pedestal or wall, where it might also be an attractive addition to a garden.

Choose a sundial with a graceful gnomon. This is a good guide to the quality of the total design. If you want to 'kink' things up a bit, hold an *evening* installation party to get the advice of friends on setting the dial correctly. Have the pedestal set firmly in place beforehand and the tools on hand to anchor the dial and its gnomon when its position has been determined.

Have a Party

As darkness falls, tape a yardstick up the diagonal line of the gnomon and then sit around with your guests until the stars come out brightly. Then find the Big Dipper in the northern sky, and from that the North Star on a line from the side of the Dipper. Then let each of your guests sight along the yardstick until it points directly at the North Star. Allow time for consultation and argument among your guests, then mark the position of the dial with chalk and leave it until morning. There is no need to tell your friends that it is difficult to be accurate with a sundial. The gnomon is set at an arbitrary 45 degrees for locations 45 degrees north of the equator. Further, it doesn't give accurate time unless you live on a time meridian—the 90th, 105th or 120th.

If precise time is important to you, you need to set the gnomon for high noon, a two-minute interval when the gnomon casts no shadow to either side—nothing but a thin line to the north, the exact width of the gnomon blade.

What a Dead Thing a Clock Is

Better we value the sundial for its ornamental and historical properties. It can give focus to a sunny space, and stand as a gesture to timekeepers and gardeners who have gone before. It is a nice relief from the clocks of our mechanized world. Charles Lamb is said to have commented, "What a dead thing a clock is—compared to the altar-like structure and silent heart-language of the old dial."

All dials are silent but most are verbal and a few verbose. Wordsworth favored a sundial that exhorted, *"Come! Light! Visit me!,"* but the Chinese thought more of the garden itself. *"Ere man is aware/That spring is here/The flowers have found it out."*

The wall dial is an American design from the famed Van Briggle Pottery. The ceramic tiles mark the hours in Roman numerals and show hourglasses in the corners, plus the signs of the zodiac round about. Wall dials should be calibrated on a test panel, on the site. The Van Briggle dial dates back to 1907 and indicates that even then there were stars, sun and moon.

The bronze dial of bird and worm is a fitting motif for a garden. It is a sculpture piece made in the 1920s by a man who signed himself E. Angela.

Some messages are downright sentimental, enough to embarrass a few. *"Light and shadow by turns, But always love."* Or *"I count only youthful hours."*

A dial in our own town strikes a sour note: *"Love makes Time Go; Time makes Love Go."*

The dial at the General Post Office in London is brusque: *Be about your business.*

The shadow can be cast in many ways, on a pedestal disc, a wall or a hollow sphere with an inner equatorial line. It can be traced on the sides of a garden portal, or a window frame.

At Glamis Castle the Scots have a monumental dial of stone with twenty-four facets to define the time precisely.

But for some gardeners this is more *time* than they wish to know. For them it is better to puff on a dandelion clock to count the hours, and let the seeds fly out with the wind.

Sketches Indicate Variety

Sundials are standard features in English gardens, but none is more forthright in its design than this pedestal dial at the Barnsley House, near Bath. It stands, moss-covered, on a pebbled terrace amid tubs of tulips and pansies in the spring. This particular dial was used in 1979 for the poster announcing the celebration of 1,000 years of gardening in England. The exhibition was held at the Victoria and Albert Museum in London, coinciding with Chelsea week.

Weather vanes

It isn't everyone who knows or cares which way the wind is blowing. In our electronic age some would say this is a small matter. Nevertheless, with an old weather vane you can gain basic information and at the same time have a fine ornament for your garden.

Although getting or making a weather vane isn't easy, the acquisition of one can be a pleasant pursuit. In recent years, through the interest of gardeners, many wind roosters have moved from old to new rooftops and from attics to garden walls. Rooftops may be windier, but gardens are breezy enough for this whirling breed. The weathercock, the eagle, and the dairyman's cow are popular themes. Because this was a special fad in the nineteenth century among rural folk, the barnyard is well represented, with lambs and pigs as well.

While the sundial is the oldest method of telling time, the vane is one of history's oldest forecast instruments. It rides freely and bravely on an upright rod, finely balanced, and swings about to face continually into the wind. The rooster, big and little, has always been a favorite weather indicator. He assumed this position by the edict of a

ninth-century pope, Nicholas I, who decreed that a cock should be mounted on the topmost spire of every church and abbey as a reminder of Peter's denial of Christ.

Henry Wadsworth Longfellow was also inspired. He took time to write of his own experience: "*He saw the gilded weathercock/Swim in the moonlight as he passed.*"

In spite of this charming word picture, the dictionary has picked up the definition of a weathercock as a fickle, changeable person. Today's society, however, has affection for this maneuvering turnabout.

If you don't particularly fancy a rooster, not even this charming young bird in the wrought iron cage, consider these other alternatives: Fish, insects, other birds and banners are traditionally favored. Horses, ships, whales and even grasshoppers are considered appropriate.

Design Your Own

If you can't find an old weather vane that expresses the real you, fashion your own of custom design, or purchase one of the many reproductions now available through art galleries and mail-order houses. Making your own design, the possibilities are endless. Wood or metal are the most typical materials. Don't worry if you think your talents are limited. Primitive and archaic designs are especially favored. But always, it is imperative that the vane be slender and perfectly balanced. The rear end must always swing away easily from the wind.

Many early pieces were made of two thin sheets of metal repousséd, and hammered into shape from the inside, and then joined together on the center seam. Others were silhouette-cut from a heavier metal. Do-it-yourselfers most often used wood, planks that were lightly carved.

Traditionally the vanes on their rods were collared with a device that marked the cardinal points of the compass. Legend has it that the word *news* springs from this source, indicating information accumulated from all directions, N., E., W. and S.

Collectors Identify Styles

Today's collectors have learned to identify pieces by artists' styles, the materials used, and the era. The kind of lettering used on the cardinal points is a further clue.

There is a sizable group of weather vane con-

gone so far as to use helicopters to snatch exceptional vanes from guarded estates. One bereft collector, with the help of a detective, traced his lost bird to a Florida mansion where it had been newly installed. The new 'owner' surrendered the piece, and the original collector bought an extra airline ticket to fly it back to New England.

A few early wooden vanes of humans were sometimes covered with scraps of fabric in 'suit'-able colors, right down to the suspenders and the buttons. Most of the cloth has worn away in the wind, but the vanes are held in high regard. A signalman vane from the southwest, a human figure with movable arms, still carries traces of old cloth and real buttons. He once topped a railroad depot where, no doubt, his arms flailed in the wind.

Williamsburg Treasures

The dairy cow once swiveled on the ridge of a barn roof. In her new home, in a garden, she seems content as cows should be, backed against a wall of ivy. Now fixed in place, she has a limited view, always pointing in one direction.

Weather vanes have fascinated people for as long as the cock has crowed. The cock now mounted on a brick gatepost still commands authority. His body is stout and his tail thin; he must have turned easily when he stood on a rooftop as chickens do.

noisseurs on the East Coast. Some have been known to purchase entire buildings in order to obtain the weather vanes on the roofs. Magazines report the harassments these collectors experience. Knowledgeable thieves have climbed to rooftops to steal prize specimens. Some have

More vanes and whirligigs

American art and folk museums are avid collectors of old vanes, primarily because they reveal the early eccentricities and craft skills of our forefathers. The Abby Aldrich Rockefeller Museum at Williamsburg has, at my last count, some sixty-nine fine originals. One item, a rooster, dates back to 1715.

The perforated rooster shown below is a puzzle to me. I wonder if the cock, when first installed, spun too fast on its rod, and its maker was obliged to take it down and cut holes in its body to reduce its wind resistance. The perforations certainly distinguish it from other birds.

The codfish and the pike, both symbols of Christianity and of the fishing industry, were favorite subjects, particularly in New England. Horses were portrayed in many roles, from harness-racing to trotting and jumping, or simply running flat out. In other instances they are shown pulling a fire engine or a country doctor's buggy.

The American Indian, the New Englander's friend, was generally portrayed in dignified poses. The peaceful warrior shown above is typical.

Civic institutions and businesses used weather vanes as identification signs: a fireman's hat on the firehouse, a locomotive on the roundhouse or a trolley on the car barn, and a quill where scholars gather. The Yankee Stadium, in

spite of its remodeling, retained its vane of a baseball and bat.

As we install vanes in our gardens we might follow tradition by selecting symbols and totems having a personal significance to ourselves or our hobbies. The butterfly or the grasshopper might be especially appropriate. The butterfly vane sketched opposite at lower right is a rare jewel. Made of brass and still shining, the vane gives evidence of mistreatment by riflemen. But somehow, in this instance, the vandalism is less an affront. The random markings seem more a pattern of Nature than the handiwork of man.

Some butterflies not only point in the direction of the wind but also flutter their wings in the breeze. While few of these are still in existence, it might be a fine time to create a modern version.

The Japanese have been as intrigued with our weather vanes as we have with the ingenious toys of their making. To satisfy this curiosity, folk art museums shipped an exhibit to Japan's World's Fair for display in the American Pavilion. It included examples of the stork, the leaping deer and the Statue of Liberty.

The angel Gabriel still blows his horn, while swinging from a three-pronged standard, no doubt representing the Trinity. Today he flies high above a forest of loblolly pine in Virginia after having spent many years on top of an early American church spire.

At the Rockefeller Museum garden an early American eagle, the inspiration for our national emblem, now sits proudly on a garden wall. Made of metal with a gold overleaf, he is impressive where he glistens among the trees.

The trotting horse and sulky was a favorite theme in the nineteenth century. It reflects the sporting pleasures of a time when the forecasting of the weather and the winds was no more scientific than a wavering weather vane on a rooftop.

Whirligigs as Toys

Whirligigs, in contrast to weather vanes, were not intended to be functional.

Whirligigs, by definition, can be any toy that is whirled, twirled or spun around. This could include a pinwheel, a top and a merry-go-round. A whirligig is also a whim, a notion and a crotchet. A crotchet, besides being a hook used in crocheting, is an odd notion, an unreasonable whim, or the ultimate whimsicality. That assures us that we are on firm ground. Here follies and conceits are the order of the day.

Whirlwigigs were made by craftsmen and whittlers for their own and family amusement. These ingenious little contraptions were designed to sit on poles in the garden where they could display their windblown antics, entertain people and ward off a few marauding fowl. With the true genius of modest men, swordsmen of wood dueled in the sun, soldiers in full dress flung their arms out in wide circles. Other figures in top hats twirled on their spinning platforms. These whirligigs were generally homemade and few have survived. However, there is a modern cult of practicing whirligig makers who make these products during the drab winter months. A man at the bottom of our hill sets out a new array each spring and by midsummer many are gone.

Wood-carvers find opportunities for self-expression in whirligig production. They carve soldiers with trim uniforms, big eyes and curled mustaches. Their arms terminate in wide paddles instead of hands. A top-hat personage may also have a long nose, a cutaway coat, and high-heeled boots. The swordsmen, to keep swinging, need a wide paddle on one arm to keep the sabre on the other flashing in the sun.

The best of the old whirligigs have been moved from fence posts into museums and there is a ready market for new designs. If you wish to commit yourself to such goings-on you might search out a charming book titled *Weathervanes and Whirligigs* by Ken Fitzgerald. In it he describes the principles of the locomotion involved and suggests many designs suitable for the home craftsperson. He also lists principal manufacturers of commercial weather vanes today.

And then, as if we weren't done with whirligigs, there is the whirligig beetle, an insect we should all remember from our childhood, a bug that swims around in circles on the surface of the water.

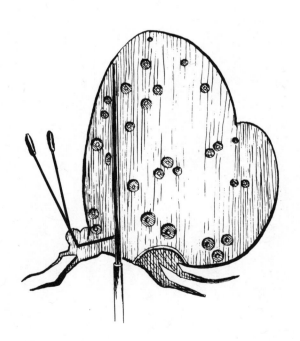

Embellishments with an old world touch

Delving into old world traditions and design concepts can have double value in your garden. It can introduce you to objects you didn't know you could love, whether for their charm, their oddity or their conversational bait. But of greater importance, these finds can suggest themes and styles on which an entire garden design can be built. Phillip Guston, a twentieth-century painter, claimed that our greatest problem in art is subject matter. "Before you can create, you need to decide what to do, and how to begin. You also need to do something worthwhile."

The Victorian grouping of children playing in the shade of an umbrella suggests the wonder and inquisitiveness of the very young. The idea itself can become the springboard for several garden designs, either period or modern in tone. The elf, standing in the boxwood, apparently was brought in from another source to complete the fable and focus the children's gaze. The fairy-like piece is set down on a broad lawn at the edge of the wide Piankitank River in Virginia's tidewater country. A few trees, a conifer and a sycamore stand out from the edge of the forest. The figures, as modeled, have a reality that is strange to modern-day sculpture, but they seem alive from another time.

The neighing horse was originally a business identification sign. It has since hung on a shed wall, making a fine ornament in the garden. But since this photo was made, the horse has gone. The boys from the local college found him to be too much of a temptation and spirited him away. He has been recovered but the owners, rather than chance another adventure, have put him in storage. There he remains, out of sight but not out of mind.

Relics in Color

The beautiful Grecian monster shown in Color Plate 24 is not a griffin, a gargoyle, or a caryatid. I'm sure there is a name for a being with a beautiful head and breasts and the body of an animal, but I don't know it. The piece was brought to this country some thirty years ago and has since rusted out in the weather. A scholar on Greek art who saw it claimed it should be back in a museum in its native land. Still it fullfilled a vital role in the garden of an American collector, bringing pleasure to all who saw it.

Color Plate 11 shows a carousel pony in the same man's garden. This he stood beside his raised flower bed. He grew geraniums and eye-level plants in the foreground and day lilies

and phlox in great clusters overhead. The pony has seen better days but she still breathes the excitement of a merry-go-round. The patina was preserved with a spray coat of clear vinyl.

Stone Treasures

This fine old piece of carved marble stands in a rose garden in Denver. It serves as a birdbath now, although it was originally a baptismal font. The carvings of deer, squirrels, birds and lions are still extraordinarily clear, and somewhat pagan in subject matter. The grapes and grape leaves seem to imply a vineyard. I also have the suspicion that the pedestal base with the dove as a symbol of the Holy Ghost is older. It is more severe in design. However, the piece in toto does make a startling ornament where it stands.

Large millstones that date back to the eighteenth century and grand plantations are still seen often in southern gardens. The one shown in the sketch was in near-perfect condition. A special platform of concrete was laid on a garden terrace as a base to raise the stone to bench height. Smaller millstones can be used as stepping stones across a stream.

With such relics from the past a thread of pleasure can form between the object and its gardener. With such entrapments, visitors will enjoy 'being there.'

Embellishments cast and recast

All that you do in your garden need not be original. If you can't create your own art objects, you can buy castings of taste and beauty from works made by others. They may be castings of objects made in foreign lands for export, castings from antique forms sold as reproductions, or castings you can develop and embellish yourself with the help of Nature.

These embellishments and refinements are intended as a pleasant exercise of your talents, not a demanding requirement upon your time. Gardening, like needlepoint, should be calming and soothing to your nerves. Both arts are intended as simple exercises that will allow you to wind down gently.

In both activities you can start with an easy project based on an existing pattern. Then, when you are ready, you can move on to more complex designs, designs that can be realized on solid ground, as on a needlepoint canvas. The instinct to advance and excel is evident in these and other avocations. The sport fisherman learns to tie his own lures and flies, the weekend runner soon aspires to marathon competition. The beginning gardener in time becomes his own 'detailer' and eventually his own landscape designer.

The Italian filmmaker, Federico Fellini, understands the trials such aspiration can bring. "Sometimes," he says, "when pulling a little tail, you find an elephant at the other end." He speaks true. Advancement is never easy. Perhaps, as gardeners, we need to be satisfied, for a while, with less, and find respite in reproductions made from others' works in our gardens.

Invention in art as we know it is little more than a new combination of familiar forms, previously gathered. If you are unable to retain these visual impressions you will have difficulty in creating new ones. What we need to do then is reuse and design from those things we do remember. We are all artists in one degree or another, chained to our memories and our minds.

While our minds are idling we can turn our attention to garden details. This too is a vital part of the whole glorious pattern of gardening.

Buy Imported Reproductions

If your garden space is strewn with giant boulders, revel in your good fortune and make no attempt to move them. Instead, fill the depressions around them with rich soil and hearty ground

covers to make a deep sea of green. Then mount a lantern on an island rock and plant a small tree close by. To this add a sculptural detail at midsea and your problem is solved.

The photo shows just such a solution, and the appointments used are fine oriental reproductions of distinguished bronze castings. They are authentic in character and superb in craftsmanship. The lantern used is a snow-scene lantern with a wide roof to shelter the light chamber. The geese are duplicates but by thoughtful arrangement they are made to seem quite different, one from the other. They are simple in line and mass.

The paved terrace in Mississippi is made from custom-made castings of concrete imprinted with the bold leaves of the aurelia plant. In another region the leaves used in the mold for the imprint might be horse chestnut, sycamore, or a small branch from a pondorosa pine. For added excitement three tiles were omitted in the center of the terrace and a large washtub countersunk in the space. A lotus lily is grown in the tub and bright red impatiens fill the spaces between. This is a project that an energetic gardener might do alone. Or one could make the hexagon mold and gather the leaves needed for the imprints, and then hire a strong boy to make the castings as a project for as many Saturday mornings as it takes to create enough tiles.

The terrace garden in the Black Forest of Colorado boasts a fine collection of cast iron stoves. These black beauties are now held in high regard for their charming shapes and their ability to produce heat when we need it. This collection predates the oil crunch, although some of the pieces have now been pressed back into service. A wide roof protects the exhibits; a white back wall silhouettes their lively forms. Green plants, including petunias and oleander, grow in between.

Embellishments of fine art

The true artist is an upsetter of established order. ''What they do,'' according to art critic Herbert Read, ''is eternally disturbing, permanently revolutionary. It is a matter of confronting the unknown, of bringing back an outward image of inward things.''

This is no doubt true in many cases, but sculptors in particular have an affinity for the garden. Perhaps because both deal with natural forms, the artist is at home in this place.

Elie Nadelman's exquisite sculpture of a resting stag is a refined portrayal. Its rounded surfaces withstand the hard light of the roving sun well. There is delight in its simple forms and a sense of intimacy. The small piece stands on a shelf in front of a greyed wall where its bronze surface shimmers in the sun.

The stag and the swans, by Gaston Lachaise, are displayed in a fine sculpture garden at Murrell's Inlet, South Carolina. The swans are of cast aluminum, and life-size. They 'swim' in a garden pond. Water movement stirs the reflections and enlivens the gleaming image. Sculptures, we are told, should be enjoyed from many aspects if we are to please ourselves and the artists who make them. A sculptural piece reflects an artist's preoccupation with a series of created profiles. It is up to us to discover them.

For many of us the excitement is in the doing, but with the professionals, concentration is on the end product, its quality and how this will contribute to his reputation. By studying these works we might see things otherwise denied us. There is some risk that it will discourage our own effort,

but this new awareness and alertness can also intensify our experience and add to our enjoyment.

Henry Moore, the famed British sculptor, has his own sculpture garden. It is planted with large trees and no flowers. He urges us to draw so we will look more carefully. He says, "I know more about trees now. . . . As a child it's two dimensional. You learn three dimensions as you grow. . . . Sculpture uses this three dimensional world, a world of force."

Moore's sculptures and drawings possess a going in, a going around and a coming back. They allow the observer to experience an idea fully. Moore recommends that you do a sculpture in a small model first. "You can turn it over in your hands. You feel like God, creating." Size for him has its own emotional impact. Like Stonehenge, which is bigger than people, you can

cal precision that suggests a culture different from our own. Here too it is imperative that we circle the area, watching the empty circles change their shapes while remaining still. These pristine pieces offer us intriguing contradictions.

The flex-steel sculpture by Chicago artist Forman Onderdonk now points the way to a wilding garden in the Rockies. The artist and the garden owner have used their separate tools as musical instruments. The sharp blades of the yucca plant seem to vibrate as from a bow. The sculpture directs our eyes to the left with force and then brings us back gently and by degrees. It seems as if this wind harp is moving. There are contrasts in textures, and contrasts in light values, but still a delicate melding.

Color Me Iridescent

The peahen by Edgar Britton, Color Plate 23, is a modest bronze designed to stand among the flowers. Her form is not so spectacular as her mate's might be but she is iridescent with bits of color, brilliant enamels that were applied and glazed on after the casting. She is lightweight enough to be moved about at whim, sometimes standing among the trollius, at other, when the flowers grow too tall, out on the lawn.

go inside and through. When people puzzle over his work he says, ''There should be some difficulty in following.''

The I-beam columns on a wild garden ridge in Littleton, Colorado, show the crisp steel forms of sculptor Robert Mangold against the softness of the plant growth. The columns have a mathemati-

Embellishments by local talent

The true purpose of art is to bring to consciousness the highest interests of the mind. This viewpoint is valid but it can scare off the budding artist or collector. High ideals are fine but many of us want a simpler interpretation. Picasso spent a decade learning what to do with blue, and then he learned how to do without it. Always we must explore new things, discover colors we had never seen before.

Picasso was challenged for jumping from one style to another. He responded, ''I never had a style. Did God have a style? He made the guitar and the dachshund.''

It's good to learn from the masters. They are firm and convincing in their views. But we can also learn from local artists. They may not speak with as much authority but they have ideas that can be helpful.

In addition to picking their brains we can buy their works. Few of us can afford the works of big names in the arts but we can support regional professionals.

Today almost every sizable town has its own art gallery. Interior decorators also keep a showcase supply of outdoor furniture and art. Artists inhabit every picturesque corner of our fair land. Most welcome your inquiries and purchases. It gets down to knowing what you want that you can afford. It may be true that beauty is in the eye of the beholder, but much depends upon what we bring to the beholding.

Search out the countryfolk who paint and carve in a primitive way. These things have special charm. While traveling along the Gulf Coast I

spied two huge trees that had been sheared of all their branches. Butchered they were, but they stood bold and beautiful because someone had painted them, top to bottom, in red, white and blue layers.

On that same day I also spotted a woodcarver's porch filled with freshly-carved and painted wooden Indians. They may never stand in front of a cigar store, but they could be just right for a certain type of garden.

The nail painting is a prickly invention of an art gallery owner in Santa Fe. It hangs on a courtyard wall by strong hooks because it is indeed a weighty object. The nails are driven into a heavy board in swirls much like the curls on an airdale. The nails change color and rust in the weather and send brown riverlets down the stucco wall. Of course it started as a novelty, but it is fun and a bit insistent. It competes with the thorny rose climber nearby.

In Taos, New Mexico, the art galleries are almost as numerous as in Santa Fe. They offer many objects and paintings of western themes. There are brilliant landscapes of New Mexico, the enchanted land so touted on license plates. There are pots from the Indian pueblos and traditional weavings. On a blue door that marks the entry into an art colony there hung a brass starburst at least four feet high that would be a delight in any garden. It appeared to be made for perforated wafers of metal welded to slender steel rod

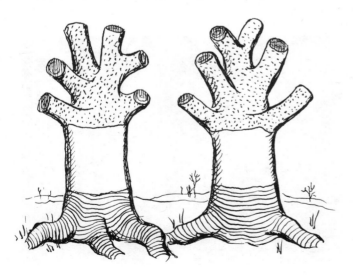

spokes. Many of the wafers were encrusted with jewel-like paints. The greatest concentration of color was in the center, and beautiful.

Hometown paintings by members of the local guild can be put to good garden use, particularly if they are weatherproofed with acrylics and matte varnish. The sunflower painting, right, on a carport wall, has all the shelter from the weather it needs. The owners decided they needed a note of bright color beside the kitchen door since most visitors came that way instead of up the front steps. The biggest hazard comes from the newspaper carrier who flings the paper across that wall each morning. This leaves scuffs of grey ink that can be washed away with a light touch and some difficulty.

Folk-art Color

The bottle tree shown in Color Plate 20 is a local project inspired by a tradition practiced in the South. Pine trees grow fast in that part of the country and the loners along the highway die quickly. It becomes a chore to dig up the standing dead, so some folks let them be and break back the branches instead. This leaves the tree with a lot of hooks that seem to beg to be hung upon. The closest things around are empty wine bottles from the roadside. These add a touch of holiday color. Next the homemaker is bringing out her vinegar and liquid bleach bottles and her husband's beer bottles. Soon the tree becomes a thing of pride. The plastic bottles have no sparkle but they remain. The tourist wagon outside of Jackson, Mississippi, passes out postcards of patchwork quilts—and of bottle trees.

With a postcard in hand and a remembrance of the trees I had seen along the highway, I decided to make a bottle tree of my own. I passed the word to friends to save wine bottles and I started saving our own. In the meantime I reshaped about five feet of wire fencing into a cone shape. As you see I had already departed from the pine branch framework. With the help of our taller son we drove a one-inch solid aluminum rod into the softened earth near the side fence. I didn't know how this was going to turn out and I didn't want my folly apparent from the front road. The rod stood out of the ground about five feet and the wire cone hung over the rod top like a Christmas tree. Then came the tedious part. With stiff galvanized wire I made hooks around the neck of each of the seventy or so bottles I had accumulated, and hung them on the cage. It took several days to make the hooks with long-nosed pliers and more time to rearrange the bottles for the best stained-glass colors. I became aware of a shortage of blue ones and sent out the word for Bromo Seltzer and milk of magnesia bottles. Without asking I received a "Quink" ink bottle that was just right near the top with all the little pharmaceutical bottles. The tree is a year-round delight although a few bottles froze and cracked during the winter. Now our younger son wants to move it to the front and put tree lights inside the cage for Christmas.

Bare facts

Let us get to the facts directly. Gardeners through history have loved the human form as a sculptural element. It is a shape that is beautifully articulated and of graceful and flowing line.

This perpetual admiration has not been empty repetition. Even before the Greeks and as far back as the Jericho of 7000 B.C. human forms have been revered. From there you can go back to Adam and Eve in the garden, not sculptured, but described in fig leaf dress.

In the golden age of Greece there was mythology with all its visual and ornamental opportunities—Venus and Adonis, Apollo and Daphne, Cupid and Psyche and Orpheus and Eurydice. The Romans followed with their own esthetic versions, always a mingling of fine sculpture and fine plants, in close company.

In the Dark Ages there was less of more, including sculptures, but by medieval times the nude was evident in walled gardens, if you can believe the old drawings and prints. The garden was also the bath, and man and maid romped together in and around the fountains, in real life, not in stone.

Topiary followed soon after as statuary's chief competitor. It is not clear whether a new morality had developed or an early depression with its lack of means had shifted ornamental design from sculptured forms to clipped shapes in holly, cedar and box. But topiary enthusiasms faded fast and stone figures reappeared in the garden. They remain popular today. What I show here is just a small sample of current directions.

The female torso has been distilled for boldness. Its voluptuous beauty is sun-modeled differently with each hour of a sunlit day. The sculpture by Albert Stewart stands in his own garden in Padua Hills above Los Angeles. Its columnar form is as strong as an ancient caryatid, and dedicated to supporting the sky.

The scabrous nude guards a small swimming pool in Colorado. She is a museum reproduction that has seen better times, but remains beautiful in her weathered masses.

Most of us acknowledge the value of such ornament in a public garden but too often deny ourselves the same privileges.

Since peopled gardens are the most-loved, it is

only natural that we would want to design with human forms. Landscape architects shape their spaces with people in mind—children on play structures, young people playing badminton or sprawling on the grass, or parents sitting together around a table by candlelight. When we don't have people around, we can use sculptures.

The Three Graces stand in a lily pond beside the Linnaen House at the Missouri Botanical in St. Louis. The life-size figures, by Gerhard Marcks, are stylized enough to remove them one step from reality. To me they are a real delight, an exaggeration of form and flow just right for a garden.

A good sculpture, the saying goes, can be rolled down a hill without breaking. This voluptuous nude should have no trouble qualifying. No bigger than a melon, it nestles comfortably in a nest of juniper. To some it may go unnoticed, no more than a rolling stone. The piece is carved from travertine, indigenous to the area. The sculptor is Edgar Britton.

The curvaceous bathing beauty was a star feature at a Chicago flower show. She stood in a latticed bower about to dive into a small lily pool. The crowds filed by, two abreast, and there was little chance for photography. My camera was getting pushed and shoved. Two nuns walking immediately behind me saw my dilemma and volunteered to slow down the line while I snapped what I wanted. Snap was the right term, the photo

has slight movement, but I offer it anyway. The white marble statue was luminous, almost with an angelic glow. But in her wet, clinging bathing suit she seems more erotic than a nude. The carving was sensitive and skillful, the work of an artist whose name I do not know.

No matter whether we are artist or observer, we should discover the magic sense of human things—the articulation of an elbow, the swell of the hipbone and the flowing line of a thigh. These images are universal.

CHAPTER FIVE

Found Art

Found art can bring playfulness into your life and your garden. For that reason alone it has great value. Wit and mirth should be among our standard garden tools. This one-of-a-kind art can be yours for the finding. Like it or not, our world is strewn with old bottles, tree fragments, architectural scraps, bones and stones that are waiting for the scavenger with a discerning eye to rescue them from oblivion. There are thousands, maybe millions, of strange items in the mountains, on the seashore, along the river banks and in the junkyards of America, waiting to be rediscovered and carried away.

Found doesn't necessarily mean *for nothing*. You often have to pay. But the find may be a great buy, just what you have needed for years—a real bargain. This could be a carpenter's weatherproof tool box to be installed on the terrace to hold the badminton set, a prize umbrella and garden hand tools. The lift-up top can be cushioned so it could double as a low seat.

It might be a strange hunk of iron that you purchased for a nickle a pound to stand at your front gate as a kind of guardian, or it could be a seashell mosaic that you made from 'jewels' you gathered and pocketed on a score of walks by the sea.

All these opportunities, all these odd shapes can take on new meaning under your guiding hand. But discovery must be yours. Enjoy the excursions and don't belittle the end product. Most objects can be twice beautiful, first to you as you find them and second to your family when viewing the finished product. But *finished* is a key word. Found art needs to be well-presented to be a true delight. Presentation is often part of the story. Oftentimes it is as important as the object itself.

Good Presentation Essential

If you take a fancy to a gnarl of wood, a fragment of iron or an architectural remnant with extraneous segments, make amputations boldly. Break off or whittle away any distracting elements. On most objects you can stain any freshly-exposed surfaces; match the faded colors of the rest of the piece as closely as possible. The best way to accomplish this on wood is with a succession of thin coats rather than one thick and generally conspicuous layer of viscous paint. With iron it is less easy. You may need several matte colors to cover the sheen and to simulate the rust and the dirt grey.

Bone-painting

If you start gathering bones, try the age-old custom of the Plains Indians: paint bone surfaces with arabesques using lamp black or natural dyes. Take a serious look at strap iron, barrel hoops and worn out horseshoes and see if you can make an elegant iron gate. Take a second look at old cook stoves, even if the grate is burned out and replacements are beyond you. Use the artful monster in your back garden as a serving buffet or party bar. The firebox can be filled with an ice chest and the warming oven above can hold glassware or food.

Delve into a river bottom after a flood to find cottonwood trees that have been uprooted and overturned. Take along your Swedish saw and trim off a group of roots that might be cut and trimmed into a wood monster. Let him leer out at guests from a shaded corner of your garden. Use the roots as limbs, pretty much as they come, but carve a face and big ears to amuse your visitors.

Even snow can be a found object. If you are having a winter party, roll a line of snowmen to bid welcome at the party hour, or lift a fat snowman, piece by piece, into the hammock you unwittingly left out too long.

Beachcombing Useful

The pursuit of the unknown, for unknown purposes, can be truly venturesome. It can take you to far places, beachcombing along the Gulf Coast for shells and glass 'pebbles', prowling the desert for bones of wild animals, or climbing to old mining sites in the mountains for weathered timber fragments, rock crystals, or twisted wood.

Even a trip across town to the ironmonger's junkyard can be uplifting enough to make your day. In your travels you will make new acquaintances at flea markets, auction houses, or auto salvage yards—plumbers unloading old pipes, lead sinks and other castoffs, auto wreckers with old tires, spare wheels and disabled gearboxes.

If you get into all this, build up a collection of wood blocks and stone slabs to use as mounts for your works of art. Small objects can be mounted by drilling two holes or more in the underside of the object and into the top surface of the block. Then pin the two parts together with stout or slender nails, depending upon the heft of the object. Remove the nail heads for easier installation. Dab a bit of super glue into each hole, top and bottom, add the nails and hold in place until the glue sets.

Feel free to combine unlike materials in weird or wonderful ways. Do it to shatter a presumed image or to respond to a strange impulse.

Use Fence Posts as Pedestals

Don't let your fence posts stand idle. They make fine pedestals for sculpture any season. Carve a bird that can sit on one, and mount a deer scapula in a strange position to pose on another. If you should have access to an old stone sink or water trough, hire a truck and bring it home. Set it in a corner and plant it with alpine flowers for an early display of fine wildings. Stay active and enthusiastic.

Century-old Pursuit

The flotsam and jetsam of coastlines have fascinated beachcombers for centuries. Irridescent mussel shells found there can be arranged in a garden as flowers, a whale's skull can be hung on a garden wall. Mountain climbers and backpackers content themselves with smaller trinkets, a perfectly round glacial pebble or a twist of krumholst juniper as a memento of a great hike at timberline. Would-be geologists gather amethyst-lined geodes to bring home and split open to enjoy their long-hidden jewels for years thereafter.

What is revealed each morning on the seashores or in the city streets is mostly classified as litter. Yet even the smelly kelp on the beach has its own enthusiastic gatherers. So why not join the horde? You, too, can become a connoisseur of the derelict; your tastes and your enthusiasms can reenshrine forlorn oddments where they can be loved and enjoyed again.

Attic treasures

When you go looking for found art, start close to home. Search the attic or cellar first. Take a second look at that old dusty reed settee with matching chairs. Clean and spray paint the reed in some wild color, fuchsia or spring green, and make up new slipcovers for the cushions in another color equally flamboyant. Then put them out on your porch or patio for instant enjoyment.

Pull from the attic trunk the old white sheets that were set aside because they were not permanent press. Tie lightweight clothes lines to their folded-down corners and use them as shade squares, tied to the house or the trees. Hang one over the children's sand pile and another over the old-fashioned double swing.

If there should be a stained-glass window in the attic wrapped in rags and standing idle, put that to new use. Design a fence or a gate in which it can be inset and you have a new family treasure. Use it as in Color Plate 12 as a double feature. By day it is a morning glory ornament in this garden entry room. By night, lighted from behind, it becomes a guide for arriving guests.

The southern California gate was especially designed to receive this diamond-shaped piece. The setting is modern and the stained-glass ornament seems equally modern. The morning sunlight intensifies the glass colors within the garden.

Stoneware Good Outdoors

If you have the beginnings of a stoneware collection, display it proudly and welcome any offers of additional pieces. The five-gallon brown jug is from Bennington, Vermont. It was considered big enough to hold a fair ration for one lap of a pioneer's journey to the West in a covered

wagon. The smaller grey jug with the salt glaze topping is from the gold-mining town of Cripple Creek, Colorado. Imprinted on the side is the information 'When empty return to the Old Kentucky Liquor House'. It was found, face down, in deep mud below the spillway of the more recent Skagway Reservoir. The brown-and-white bean jar and vinegar jug are standard items.

While you are looking close to home, salvage an old bicycle wheel to build a whirligig. This they do in Amana, Iowa, to keep the birds out of the orchard and the vegetable patch. The wheel is mounted high on a post in the thick of the plants and discs of color are inserted between the spokes. As the wheel spins, the colors blur and the birds are unnerved. Even if it doesn't keep the predators away, it makes a fine ornament in a garden.

One year we used plastic pinwheels from the dime store to keep the robins out of our strawberry patch. It wasn't very effective but fortunately there were enough berries for all of us. We did hear later that pinwheels, stuck in the ground over molehills, will send the animals packing. It is not the colors but the vibrations in the ground, made by the stick, that the moles object to.

Getting back to bicycles, pick up a pair of handlebars and an old leather seat and mount them together as Picasso once did to make a young bull's head.

Playfulness Is for All

For Picasso his artistic and personal life were one and the same. He did magnificent paintings and he also put together strange things, in playful ways.

He put two toy cars together, bottom to bottom, to make a baboon with her young. He used pitcher handles to make the ears and a strip of metal to make the tail. He used a baby carriage as the base for a bronze casting. The baby within wore a bonnet that was a piece of fluted pottery, and its limbs were made of curved pipes. He made masks and animals of cardboard and then had them transferred to sheet metal. This paper-thin material was quickly transformed into a substantial work of art.

He was forever playful, taking a curvaceous pot from the pottery while the clay was still pliable and punching and poling it until it became a standing female with elongated proportions. Once he started with a dressmaker's dummy and added a head and arms to make an exceedingly prim

lady. Always there was room for fantasy, whimsy and earthiness. These are elements that do well in a garden. Most of us enjoy the comic but need an excuse to bow to it. Wit for many people is a suppressed art. We all need a place to laugh in the sun.

Except for the entertainment centers, there are few places we can build frivolously except in a garden. Architecture, by tradition or edict, must be durable, serious and long-lasting. Where but in a garden could we build a playpool for children with a rustic trellis overhead to hold shade-giving vines? Only on the downspouts at the outer tips of a cathedral has the humor of gargoyles been allowed. How many of us, when the opportunity has arisen, have felt daring enough to play in a maze or a labyrinth? We should not waive our basic rights to playfulness. We must not leave this pleasure to the entertainers and the eccentrics.

Build a wine cellar as a summer-long project. Dig it deep and roof it over well. Then make it sparkle with color by adding bottles imbedded in the concrete dome.

Old iron

If scavenging gives you qualms, concentrate instead on scrounging in junkyards where, if they let you in, you can buy trivialities from the owner at ten cents a pound if you weigh them yourself. We once went in looking for something I have since forgotten, but we found a sawed-off endpiece of a three-feet-wide boiler. The end was rounded and had a heavy rim. In fact, the whole thing was very heavy, weighing something over a hundred pounds. Together with a kitchen dolly that originally was used at hotel conventions for serving up 500 portions of mashed potatoes at a time, the two pieces give us a movable firepit which we use on the terrace on cool summer nights.

My favorite example of a well-used discard is this salvaged and assembled ornament. It was placed in a grove of live oak trees on a high promontory overlooking the Pacific, at Nepenthe. While waiting for our luncheon to be served, I ducked outside to photograph the piece. When I returned to the table Guy said, "You looked like a typical tourist." I took this as a compliment because that's what I think I am. I love to see new places, and I am forever looking for new garden ideas. Upon leaving the place I spotted one more

exotic excursion with salvaged materials, a birdfeeder made from a wheel cover and an expanded gearbox. It also was a lantern at night. I snapped that picture too but again I hurried too fast and overexposed my subject. Let a sketch at least explain the design.

The ornament I photographed is a green glass Japanese float that found its way to California shores. The rings are of heavy ship iron bolted together and onto its redwood base. The orb and the rings are jewel-like in a good setting.

The boiler monster on page 120 stands as a guardian beside a garden gate in Aspen, Colorado. Its water coils, vents, nuts and bolts give evidence of its complexity. Visitors examine it closely and grope for information on its significance. The owners are evasive in their explanations. I suspect that they see no point in explaining a wonderful joke.

A time clock graces the wall of a retirement home, the same home that has the tree wells on the rear terrace. The piece serves as a kind of celebration of freedom from pressing engagements or daily commitments. A cantilevered bench below it is angled for greater comfort and better drainage. A detailed view is shown elsewhere.

The fine wrought iron fencing was brought down from a rooftop terrace where a widow once walked. It was mounted on a used brick wall just two feet high, enclosing a streetside paved terrace. Vines climb the parkway tree and *Pachysandra* greens up the edges. New Orleans furniture was ordered by mail and painted with a matte black to match the fencing.

Salvage opportunities

Whether you're collecting found art or salvage, a little forethought goes a long way. A friend has a cache of large stones that she has gathered with the help of her husband over many years. They walk river banks where the stones are waterworn and well polished. From each weekend excursion they bring back one or at most two stones. In their minds the stones have names and identify the place where they were found. First they are collected for their beauty, but in time they are used in their garden as stepping stones or to support a weak stem or press another into straighter growth.

People who live up in the high country pick up the scraps of iron they find when climbing the high ridges. The miners who roamed this country and staked claims a hundred years ago were as careless as today's tourists. With no transportation except a tired mule, they traveled light and discarded anything that was no longer essential. Bits of iron can be found in fern-filled canyons and on mountain screes. Sometimes it is a matter of whether you are mule enough to carry it out.

Everyone has favorite forms—spheres, cones, cubes or cylinders. Our older son admires the helix. He saw it most often as a boy, pushing the lawn mower. On all models, from hand-powered to gasoline-driven, the helix-type blades are beautiful. This beauty is often ignored because the blade is so utilitarian. Recently the family mounted an old mower upright on a six-by-six post, to turn lazily in the wind. It doesn't turn that well but we like it. We also like the idea that it relates to the DNA molecule and the chain of life. We like it too in winter, when the frosts build up.

Hitching posts today either stand at the curb in fine old neighborhoods or get pulled up and junked. Most are fine works of art. The vintage post shown here is colonial and of graceful line. It stands beside a roadway in Virginia, once utilitarian, now an eighteenth-century work of distinction.

Ideas are so fixed in our minds that a hitching post not shaped like a horse is quite unsettling. One day I spied a dog's head, a water spaniel, on a post. It was well drawn and of excellent line but it seemed an affront to tradition, and who would dare to do that?

Horses and Luck

The craftsman or artist who designed the metal ribbon gate dared to be different, even frivolous.

sell casually to interested parties for mad money. (Sometimes the customers are mad too; some are preservationists who are frustrated because they were unable to protect the structure.)

When we first came to town we rented a seventeen-room house with golden oak, mahogany, and bird's eye maple paneling and sliding doors with handsome brass hardware. The house had been the community's first mortuary, and when we rented it, it was owned by the city. Within a year it was condemned to make room for a wider street and the word got around quickly. While the main floor was still our private abode, we were beseiged by snoopers checking over the opportunities. Going into our bedroom one day, I found a strange woman walking about. She smiled and explained, "It's all right, I'm checking the doorknobs."

The stone acanthus ornament is set in a new brick garden wall in Old Town, Chicago. This is the same garden with the hand-carved double doors shown in the section on gates. The acanthus stone is somewhat distressed, but still shows evidence of its original beauty. The plaque faces the public sidewalk and lends distinction to the new wall.

Wisely he started with a rigid iron frame and several wheel rims or barrel hoops. To this he added grass-like ribbons and numerous spirals to fill the spaces and to blur public view into a rear garden. Over the gate and connected to the fence posts he arched a series of worn horseshoes, with most of the luck running out. A horseshoe on a wall or over a door, I've been told, is not lucky at all unless the tips face upward and the shoe serves as a cup to hold the luck in. If we are going to be superstitious we had better go all the way and learn how to make things work to our benefit. Never throw a hat on a bed or rock an empty rocker, or you're in trouble!

How to Acquire

Architectural remnants are better acquired if you have connections. It helps to be an architect yourself, or a housewrecker with an eye for beauty instead of profit. Of course if you haunt the storage yards at the end of the day or catch the man who flings the wrecking ball you may come up lucky. Watching the paper for announcements of upcoming houserazings can point you in the right direction. On a special building of architectural merit, the workmen sometimes take down a stone-faced facade, piece by piece, and lay the best pieces in a line at the back corner of the lot to

Beautiful bones

As Georgia O'Keefe discovered long ago, there is something stark and exciting about greying calcified remains. From femur to phalanger, from dust to dust, bones are particularly sculptural and distinctive additions to a garden. This is a found art widely practiced by western gardeners.

Appreciation of these forms goes back a long way. The Indians of the Great Plains had deep admiration and reverence for these evidences of earlier generations of man and animal. The Denver Natural History Museum shows examples of buffalo vertebra painted in arabesques.

An artist friend is equally captivated. He embellished the horse's skull in the tradition of our land's earliest inhabitants. He also combines scraps of bone with enameled metals to create bird-like creatures to grace his garden.

Our friend enjoys gathering bones with special sculptural attributes. "Like Georgia O'Keefe, I've always been attracted to the patina of rusted iron and bleached bones." He has a pair of buffalo skulls hung in a shadowed corner where the hairline tracery of the skulls can be studied at leisure.

We also have deer antlers in our garden which we use to shield or brace new seedlings. They seem to have more character than a painted stake and their whiteness makes them clearly visible, to protect the plants further.

To Guide Your Way

Bone, like white marble, has one other use. When placed beside a gate or a path, it serves as a luminous marker or guide when you are walking around the garden in the dark.

Medieval gardeners had still another refinement. Living at a time when roast leg of mutton was standard fare, they were overburdened with as many sheep shanks or leg bones as we once were with pop bottles. To deal with the surplus they used them to edge their flowerbeds. The narrow part of the bone was buried up to the knee joint or the great trocanter. It was a knobby decoration and, like our bony ornaments, it must have glistened in the moonlight. We could use wine bottles, buried bottoms up, until the wine industry starts offering deposit returns on empties.

One of the most poetic uses of bones in my recollection was an assemblage of cattle vertebrae arranged as birds in echelon formation on the outside wall of a rustic cabin in the mountains.

I remember an opossum skull I came upon on a walk. The teeth appeared to be a brilliant orange, but there was sinew and fur still on the skull. Because of a case of bubonic plague in our area, and a warning not to touch dead animals, I left the skull where it lay. I returned the next year to gather my treasure, going to the same area, the same tree in the same ravine, but I was unable to find the skull.

Sculpture from Scapula

On another day we came upon a deer skull, complete with antlers, again on our land. Some poachers had killed the animal, butchered it on the spot, and left the head to the insects and the ravages of winter. After the shock of discovery and a fit of rage against the trespassers, we brought the beautiful piece back to the cabin as a wall ornament, and a bow to the deceased.

The deer scapula, purchased one day at a rock shop, has been the making of a small sculpture for a fence post. In turning the object in my hands it seemed most often to look like a robed person in

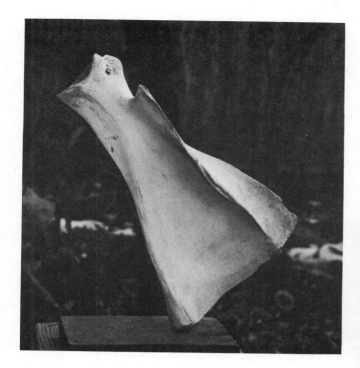

But this was still not the end. The vertebrae further down the spine were sturdier and more boxy. Individually they looked like trained dogs sitting on their hind legs. I discovered I could glue these together in groups to make what looked like a circus act piled up three or four dogs high. These trinkets made Christmas gifts for close friends who are tolerant of my aberrations. I also discovered that the shoulder blades of the turkey, fitted together in reverse, make an angel for a tree ornament. Sometimes I wonder what I might do with the bones of an ostrich.

flight. Perhaps it takes some visualization, but that is the way we mounted it, with one pin at the bottom point and into the block. The eye we added, a chip of mica, and I painted the mouth opening with some dark red dye.

The big trick is to think of bone as beautiful, not ghoulish, and to delight in it where you find it. Marvel at the enterprise and discernment of a seacoast gardener in Gordo, California, who brought a whale's skull and vertebra up to his clifftop garden to hang on a deck railing. It certainly made a unique ornament.

Turkey Bone Art

Some would say there is no accounting for taste, and I would agree, as long as you allow me to pursue this elongated and polished art. One Thanksgiving when we had an especially large turkey, I made a soup with the left-overs. The soup was good but I still had bones, beautiful, translucent fragments that I hated to part with. So, while the family was out, I boiled the bones again, this time with liquid bleach, and this time the aroma was not so aromatic. Then I let the bones drain on paper towels until they became hard and brittle again. The bones of the vertebra looked like kneeling figures, and the chest cavity like a cathedral. I mounted the 'cathedral' on a wood block and put the worshipers inside. It seemed a fitting end for a Thanksgiving bird.

Shells and stones

Shell collecting is a natural habit among seacoast people. There are so many shells cast up on the shore each day that they have become common currency in many lands—in Bermuda they have been used to build highways. The cowrie shell is ready-made for human use. In Africa and India, it needs only to be strung and worn in a necklace to give proof of great wealth. But to the garden artist it is a gift from the sea of brilliant hue and iridescence.

The patterned display of mussel shells arranged as petaled flowers on black river pebbles makes clear to me what garden art is all about. It seems a matter of capturing beauty from strange or alien elements to use in the company of growing things.

Sometimes there is fun to be found in arranging these elements in a manner that will jolt people from their set ways. It doesn't matter if it shocks or outrages others. In time it may propel them toward follies and arrangements of their own. It is fun to develop vibrations, to live in snatches, and to play with fragments.

What we experience in a garden is mild compared to what we see on a highway, in a hospital or a jail. At home no force is exerted against us, nothing is intense, nothing violent. Therefore the art we produce should rightly be mild and gentle. Fine color, easy comfort and light laughter are sufficient rewards.

At the start I admitted that this was a book of follies and conceits, of wit and personal whimsy. These stated goals have no great significance, they merely suggest areas of departure we may have missed.

We function in our own funhouse, as free as air, and we create our own hall of mirrors. Life as we live it is a blur, a scattering of impressions, and faded memories.

Shells and stones are not all bits and pieces. Giant clam shells can become basins for a fountain. One large stone can be balanced upon another to produce a state of continued apprehension.

With the building of a dam, the stone in the photograph would have been destroyed. It is a layer of rock that had lain in a stream bed for centuries, where it was carved and shaped by swirling water currents. Instead it was lifted intact and trucked into town to stand against a wall for a few more centuries. The stone was set on a concrete base and braced with junior I-beams attached to the back, out of sight. Its rounded forms and circle indentations suggest some prehistoric Henry Moore. The century plant, *Agave americana,* with its sharp blades brings almost too much contrast to the scene.

Brick, shell and stone are combined in a flowerbed border at Colonial Williamsburg. Fossilized scallop shells are arranged on a bed or crushed rock between two rows of brick edging around a bed of poppy anemones, *Anemone coronaria, A. fulgens,* and *A. hortensis,* all spectacular bulbous plants for spring. The fossilized scallops are gathered from the marl banks that built up on old coastlines.

What 'art' we do can be as a flowing river, bringing satisfaction at every bend. Striated stones and brain coral in a splash block brings pleasure while fulfilling an ordinary mission—rainstorm control. What we do may not be innovative, but if it softens an edge or adds a touch of color it will be enough for now. We are simply taking time out from the ills of the world. It is our attitudes that count. "Art," according to Oscar Wilde, "is not a thing. It is a way."

Old wood

Who would, if he could, be against wood? It is such a fine, mellow material, with the feeling of growth forever within it. It is not a rare item; it is generally available at little cost and with little effort. Wood grows to maturity in deep forests and along city streets. In our gardens we would hate to harvest it because it is more valuable to us alive and well.

There is an intimate quality to weathered wood. Like an old friend, most of it has been around for a long time. These are friendships that go back many years. A weathered cube of pine, some twelve-by-twelve-by-twelve inches in size, was found on a hillside in a nearby mining camp and brought down to us for use as a base for an ornament. For some eight years it served its purpose well. But last winter in a sharp frost, the wood suddenly disintegrated. We then picked up the fragments in a bushel basket for drying and eventual burning. This year on a chill night when spring was trying to come in, we brought the pieces in for a quick fire. The wood responded nicely, ignited quickly and burned long. As we watched the fire we speculated on the wood's age. The first gold rush at Cripple Creek was in 1890. A pine tree old enough to yield a twelve-by-twelve beam on that dry land would have started growing about fifty or sixty years earlier. That meant that we were watching a 150-year-old relic burn down to an ash. The thought was saddening, but the fire was bright and the room warmer.

The garden ornament we call our "Dancing Torso" is proof that some people produce art without realizing it. A local tree specialist, felling a green ash for us, sliced the trunk into twenty-

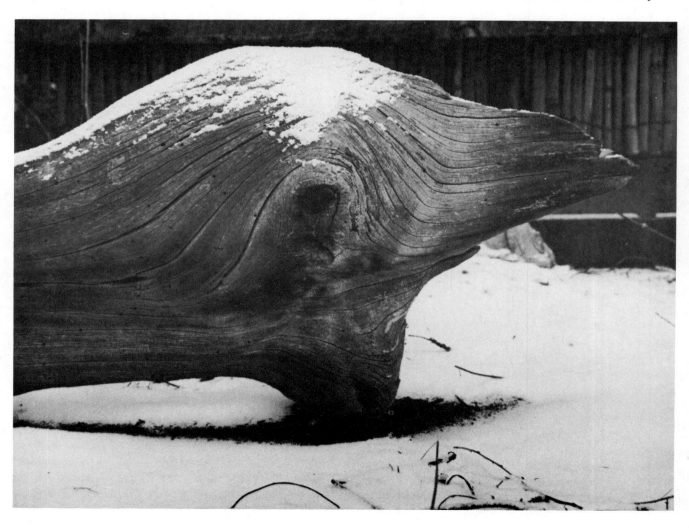

inch segments to fit our fireplace. While watching him work we noticed that one chunk of wood had a particular vitality that merited preservation. It looked like a headless Venus, with one arm flung forward as if in a dance. We rescued the damsel from a fate worse than death and stood her on a stone slab beside the marjoram plants. She waltzes all summer and continues her dance in an ermine wrap when the snows come.

The fish-board on the wall we acquired from another unaware artist. While building a breezeway between our cabin and the boys' bunkhouse, we purchased pine boards from a mountain sawmill. In the shipment was a slash of pine which we liked well enough to hang on a fence. Months later a sharp wind came up and tore the board down. It cracked and broke in a place or two, but to us it looked better than before. Now we claim that it is definitely a fish, and we have it mounted on hooks from a wire. Double hooks keep it from shifting, and we like the light reaching in behind it.

For us, wood is a familiar companion. We use a twisted branch as a tripod to hold the garden hose and direct the spray toward a particular plant. A small branch with a snake-like head we tuck under the aubretia to startle our guests.

Find a Garden Mascot

Another example is our snowy whale which we also call our Loch Ness monster. This friendly creature stood in a rear corner for many years.

His sorrowful eye followed every passerby all winter long. In spring, as if to rest, he retreated behind the tulips and by summer submerged himself among the perennials. One year he disappeared. We do not know if he was taken away as a trophy or as firewood. We have missed him.

Lessons from Nature

Collecting found art can be doubly valuable for the budding artist. What you learn from bone, stone, wood and iron can be useful to you in any medium. The sculptures we produce may not be as round as a stone, but they should have 'stone' properties. In addition to complying with the rule that they should roll down a hill safely, they should also be so formed that if you pour water on the top of each one, they will get wet all over. Why not make this simple test with your own creation?

The stones you carve yourself should have the same smoothness and flowing lines as the water-worn slab shown on a previous page.

Once you work with mussel shells and their glorious iridescence you may be tempted to try enamel work on metal, producing iridescence in a man-made form. The color plate (23) of the bronze peahen suggests the kind of embellishment possible.

The sea and the mountains offer us many kinds of magic. They reveal lines, textures and forms that should inspire you, and reappear in your own creations.

As you develop your designs don't stray too far from what Nature already produces by her own hand. Develop your ability to recognize her own art products, to discover her magic. Continue to study found art—dead twigs, live leaves, and tall trees. Work with little pieces and little ideas. Discover, in a charred fragment of driftwood, the shape of a snail that has been freed from his shell. Bring home a polished piece of mesquite, scooped from a sandy arroyo, and determine whether the twig you hold looks more like a roadrunner or a sparrow. Collect a wormy fragment of hardwood from the Connecticut shore, turn it about once or twice, and discover the ruffled baby robin that its form defines.

Investigate the strands of thin wood in an old tree stump that has been ravaged by carpenter ants. Lift out the long, fragile pieces of wood from the stump, blow off the 'sawdust' and turn them over carefully so they can be studied on their flat base—the original sawcut that created the stump. Arrange and rearrange the fragile parts until they please you, then glue them as they stand to a wood mount. If you find in these fragments the same qualities that we discovered, you will have a filigree city of great beauty and an inspiration for new creations of your own.

Pull a comb-like piece of timber from the surf and recognize the harp shape within. Then gather tiny jeweled shells from the same shore and use them to encrust the harp after you have mounted

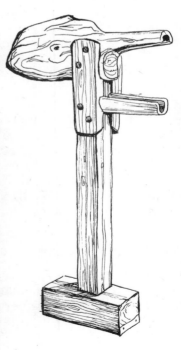

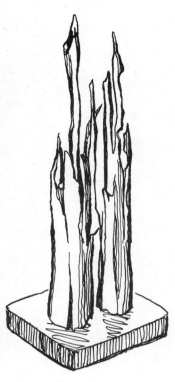

it. One piece inspires another and this is particularly helpful if you are short on ideas of your own.

A snake-like piece of twisted juniper we pulled from the Colorado River near Moab is a fine memento of an exciting boat trip in that area. But at the same time the snake shows us how slithering movement can be portrayed simply.

A woman from Tiburon Island in San Francisco Bay gathered a bucketful of stones, big and little. They were no more than a bucket of stones until she brought her own ideas to them. By sorting and arranging, by piling up and pinning down, she created a congregation of gulls that was very pleasing. The addition of a driftwood log as a platform gave the assemblage authority, and showed more strongly her intention. The rule to 'work with confidence' is golden in this case.

Most of the landscapes we see in Nature are haphazard and unlike what might be contrived by a landscape designer. The trees are not arranged to a plan. They establish themselves. A grove of aspen may develop in an awkward way because a rock strata below has shifted the flow of water and growth in that ravine. The random distribution of trees may not be picturesque as a designer might make it for an estate or a golf course, but it can have a vigor that can be gained in no other way.

In the same manner a wood sculpture of

driftwood fragments, made by an artist and gathered on a particular day along a mile of shoreline, can acquire an excitement the assemblage wouldn't have had if it were started with a preconceived notion before the artist left home. Perhaps this is why artists who pursue accidental results have good days and bad days. This is a frustrating approach to design, but still, the good days can be better for a particular artist than if all work was controlled and according to a plan.

CHAPTER SIX

Improvisations

Now that the genie is out of the bottle and creativity is yours to command, do a little improvising. Do what you want with what you have or what you can get. This is the tool of the free spirit, to be used with caution or abandon, according to your nature.

The framers of the Constitution promised us happiness or at least the pursuit thereof. We should take this offer seriously, savor the possibilities and make our choices. It is time for new departures.

Find a Way

If you need a bridge across a ravine or a ditch and you lack the money for stout underpinnings, reach out to an existing tree and use it as a support to get to the other side. If you haven't the funds for planks and railing, go rustic and find poles in some farmer's creek bottom, get his permission to take them out, for a price or a song. If you can get rope but no planks, build a three-rope suspension bridge from bank to bank so you and your agile friends can walk one rope while holding on to the other two.

If you crave a dramatic feature in your garden and you have no stone, no iron and no stout chunks of wood, scrounge around for some sailcloth and poles and assemble a sail sculpture like the one on page 140 by Peter Gourfain. tie sheets of cloth to pointed stakes and push the points into softened ground. Group the units in a clearing for a special party, and move them to a shaded alcove for day-to-day enjoyment.

Your sculpture may not be as dramatic as the one conceived by the original artist, but the results should please you and send you on to other adventures. If the sailcloth and stakes would be difficult to come by, stretch a clothesline between two trees, high up, and hang lengths of colored cloth, pennants, and banners to float in the wind over your party guests.

It Needn't Be Museum Caliber

Don't be discouraged if what you produce is not of museum caliber. As long as it adds brilliant color to the scene and captures the sunlight, it will be worth doing.

Assemble and unite alien parts, to make a bench or shape a wall panel. Put unlike items together, if for no other reason than that they give you pleasure so combined. Nail up a crazy fence of scrap materials, your way and for your reasons.

You have the support of scientists who claim that flights of fancy away from logical thinking develop new insights and new strength. So be it. But even if we do not find instant enlightment in our gardens, we should have a good time trying.

Arrange your garden comforts around a large tree. If you like the idea of a treehouse for yourself, get to it. Build a winding staircase around the treetrunk to carry you upward in elegant style, and to a platform large enough for a lounge, a desk and a chair. If you choose, let whimsy reign. Add a Tarzan swing for a quick descent, or a dumbwaiter that coasts on a pulley to the kitchen door for short-order requests. Plant the garden with jungle-type growth around a small clearing and grow mushrooms, berries and asparagus to eat raw.

Consider a Pool

If you want a sunken pool, dig it, but don't get carried away. A gardener in Kansas City decided that a pool would be just the thing to look down

on from his backyard deck. He started modestly on a long weekend but was soon interrupted by a friend who had just had a big argument with his wife. The gardener offered his friend a shovel to vent his frustrations, and dig he did. He soon exceeded the depth planned for the small pool but was unable to stop. He threw the earth up on the side to make a berm and decided to do a sunken terrace, twice as wide, with a flight of brick steps and a bench to make the pit convenient. The project continued for several days, and included a recirculating pump traveling through a waterfall beside the steps, ferns on the new embankment and water plants in the pool. By the time they finished, the pit was about eight by ten feet and at least shoulder deep. The gardener admits they got carried away, but he likes the end product and his friend is feeling much better.

If you fancy yourself as prim, build a geometric garden. Use those old oak boards you bought for the cabin you decided not to build to edge a cruciform garden. Define four paths leading to a center fountain, dial, or topiary. Develop any specialty that pleases you and if you can't rightly decide, work up two or three likely possibilities. Your true preference will soon be evident. The only restrictions you need to follow are those you impose yourself.

Make It New Each Year

A Denver retiree builds a totally new annual garden each year with new flowers and new colors, sometimes with additional beds and new arrangements. For the Bicentennial everything was red, white and blue in petunias, daisies, and ageratums. The crab apples that year were a bright red too as though this also was especially planned. Each year's project takes great energy but gives the garden an air of bubbling excitement. Such a process is a lot more invigorating than the practice followed by many gardeners who buy a few flats of the same kind of petunias each year and then spend the rest of the summer muttering about the dullness of gardening.

Don't ever just cut down a tree and then try to decide what to do with it. Decide first how best to use it. If two trees are crowding each other, decide which one you wish to keep and then figure out how you can use the wood in the other to good advantage. Use slices of the cut tree to pave the area around the other. Use the larger branches to make a rustic bench around the standing tree, or cut the stump high enough to serve as a pedestal for a table top. If you are cutting down two trees close together, cut them at seat level and run a bench plank from stump to stump. Digging up stumps is a big job so avoid it where you can. Make a split-level cut as shown on Color Plate 6, or gouge out the stump to make a planter or a garden wastebasket.

If you want to arch some vines over a gate, use a six-foot strip of aluminum metal from side to side and wrap the metal with clothesline so that new shoots are protected from the heat of the metal. Plywood strips can be bent well enough, but they splinter quickly. By the time the rope rots, the vines will be thick enough to provide their own shade.

I think of improvising as a talent that comes naturally to a few, a skill learned in time by the eager, and an opportunity lost by many. Perhaps I don't know when to stop on ingenuity, but if I had my druthers, I would solicit a promise from you that you would try a little improvising in your garden. If you fail, who will know? And if you succeed you will have opened up a whole new area of expertise.

Improvisations . . . alternate uses

Improvising pushes your skills toward finding new uses for old objects. It forces you to be inventive, to develop new whimsies or recreate old follies. All these are things that, were it not for the improvising, might never have happened at all. Improvising also saves you money and builds up new worth. It lets you take secret pride in your own ingenuity and allows you the advantages derived from accidental results.

If, by chance, someone presented you with a carousel pony you would need to find a way to use it in your garden. By mounting it under the trees in a back corner you could enjoy its presence and observe the children in your life as they enjoy it even more fully. With one solution, such as this, your reputation as an improvisor could become established and you could become the recipient of all manner of gifts, some useful, and some not so useful.

A friend dumps a load of hardwood turnings beside your garage door because he heard you like old stair railings. It then becomes necessary for you to use them well.

If you buy a load of firewood, neatly cut, and then, with the big party coming up, you don't know what to do with it, think smart. Wrap up bundles of wood with a length of stout wire or wrapping metal and create new seating accomodations for your guests.

Get Out Your Switchblade

If you live in the inner city where plant containers cost an arm and a leg and old tires on wheels are

junked in every vacant lot, get out your switch-blade and cut out a zigzag line from the edge of the tire tread. Cut it deep and cut it all the way through. Then reverse the rubber on the larger half. You end up with a large plant container with just enough drainage through the wheel housing to keep annual plants, set in black dirt, healthy and happy. But set the containers in place before you add the soil because they will be heavy. If this is a roof project use a fifty-fifty mix of soil and vermiculite, and stand the containers on heavy planks at right angles to the roof rafters for safety.

A couple from Denver took time out at the end of a difficult day paving their terrace to design a still life for a fenced corner. They hung the steering mechanism of an old sled on the fence and mounted one of their work gloves, still wet with concrete, on a slender rod over a round tree cutting. The vines grew quickly and the sled ornament still raises a few eyebrows, but the owners are pleasured with their monument to a hard day's work.

Hide a Roof Garden

Improvising can be used in big projects as well as little ones. A businesswoman in Aspen bought an old three-story brick building in the heart of the downtown area. With the help of an architect, she remodeled the first floor as her business quarters, the second floor as her living quarters, and the third floor as a brick-walled roof garden. A new roof was installed above the second floor and a deck built over that. The third floor roof was removed and the space left open to the sky. The outside walls were braced as necessary with arbor-type structures. From the street the structure appeared to retain its landmark look, but new uses had made it possible to preserve it.

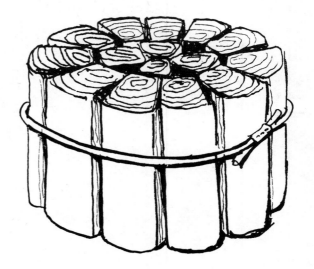

Special places

Be nimble. Respond to your own instincts. Give yourself a chance or you will have denied yourself. Put yourself in a position to be influenced by odd situations, weird weather or nosy neighbors. Accept surplus materials that people might offer you. Attack these challenges with spirit and marvel at the products you were pressured into making.

If the place you garden is hotter than the hinges of hell, build a cave on a hillside, even if you need to burrow in alone. Shore it up and bring in a chair or a cot and revel in the sudden coolness. Plant the entry with aloe and agave, and grow a Palo Verde to arch overhead. Add stones all around to protect the roots of the plants from the heat and define a path to the cave's entry. Add to the mystery by obscuring what is inside, even if this is nothing more than a shovel and a rake. Just the hint of a cave like the one on page 138 in Superior, Arizona, can amuse your guests.

If a grotto seems easier to do than a cave, dig into the side of a hill, form a chamber, stabilize the walls and roof of this alcove with chicken wire and cement, and embellish the surface with chips of quartz crystals from the local rock shop to make it glisten. Add a pool and some dripping water. Be patient, work in easy stages.

Escape to the Roof

If you live in the center of town, in an old building with nothing to garden but your houseplants, arrange to get roof privileges. Bring your plants up top for the summer and build a redwood frame with many compartments to attach to a north-facing wall. Set one or more plants in each compartment where they should thrive on the bounce light off the roof and what little direct sunlight they will get in early morning and late evening. Save rainwater if you can for watering or tote it up from your apartment. Add a lightweight wooden deck for your lounge chairs to keep from damaging the roof. The garden illustrated is in a Texas border town, a hundred feet from the Rio Grande. Because the grid is demountable it can be moved if one changes residences.

There is nothing more serene than a place where a big hammock can be stretched out between two trees. If you have several big spruce trees that have grown together as one, reclaim the center space as your own. Trim back the inside

branches to make room for the hammock and shape a narrow 'tunnel' to the center that only you will know. Use a stringed hammock because it collects neither needles nor dust, and waits on your pleasure. Flake out when you can and enjoy the birds in the branches and the clouds in the sky. You can even be smug if you want.

Some retreats can be extremely modest—a bench to sit upon among the ferns. The place should be cool and the shadows cast by the fern almost hypnotic. If the shadows please you, you might add a few more varieties of fern close to the wall. If you are the type that feels compelled to work, bring the garden hose to the bench, turn the nozzle to soft-spray, and water the ferns.

Childhood Retreats

The first garden retreat I made use of was below ground. It was a 6′×6′ concrete box large enough to hold the pump for the well at our summer cottage. Descent was tricky through a 2′ x 2′ opening and down a wall ladder, but when the weather in Illinois climbed to a sticky ninety, the descent was well worthwhile. I would let a folding chair down on a rope, put a book in my pocket and sink into the coolness for hours. I left the trapdoor open for light, and the heat never came in. I was cool but never collected. One day I hurried up the ladder to answer a call from a friend and cracked my head on the concrete ceiling. I've been the same ever since.

I think I have already mentioned our moose nest tree, under the spruce, as a cool place in Colorado, and the bamboo circle in Texas that was cooler than its surroundings. But the second place wasn't all that good. The bamboo stems knocked together in the wind and made spooky noises which distracted from my reading. Still

bamboo is a glorious plant, like no other. Its tall stems are feathery and the foliage clean cut. A cluster of large shrubs makes a picture of great beauty, just right for the subtropical garden.

One day while garden-hunting in California, I discovered that my hostess was discarding a bundle of five-foot bamboo stalks. I volunteered to unburden her and brought them back to Colorado in the station wagon. Since then I have used them every year, to coax the clematis to a new shape, to stiffen the delphiniums and to block the way when I was closing off a path.

Odd ornaments

For some housekeeping is a mess-cellany, a bunch of leftovers that need to be junked monthly. But for others, mostly gardeners, there's gold in that pile of debris.

Who, we wonder, would throw out an old sewing stand, simply because it lacks a machine, or a bowling ball simply because it is no longer capable of making strikes? Or who would burn up a bundle of choice applewood branches when they could just as well spend the winter whittling each piece into a bird-shaped stake to mark the corners of a flowerbed?

And what wasteful person would throw away that heavy black plastic tubing from the old sprinkling system when they might cut it into short lengths to pipe water down to the roots of asparagus and rhubarb in the back corner of the vegetable garden?

Mostly it is fun to discover ways to use familiar things in new places—a cluster of fine hardwood shoe trees now assembled as ducks on a rail at the edge of a pond, or photographic developer tanks being used as plant troughs and packed with moss around summering houseplants.

Now, with the help of superglue, you can try a ceramic piece. Raid the back china closet for odd bowls and dishes, a teapot or sugar bowl with side handles, a butter cover and the like. Stack them on upward into a tall figurine and when you have an arrangement that pleases you, glue the parts together permanently. Arrange bowls and saucers upside down so they will shed water. Then plant your whimsy behind the lobelia and in front of the zinnias.

From Francis Bacon to Pablo Picasso you have backing for such excursions. Bacon said, ''There is no excellent beauty that hath not some strangeness in the proportion.'' Picasso advised, ''Open yourself to the invention of art, its wonders and potentials for you.''

Incorporate a large chessboard in your square-tiled terrace paving. Then shape the pieces from timber scraps, six-by-six and four-by-four sawings, double- and triple-stacked. Your children can learn the game while they move the pieces for you and your spouse as you play.

Make a coat hanger mobile and hang it with bits of colored glass to glint in the sun. Collect one-of-a-kind drinking glasses and candle stubs, and assemble them as hurricane lanterns. Stand them on the fence frame for use at an evening party.

Build a ruin on the highest mound in your gar-

generosity of local opticians. Included are bifocals and trifocals, clear and tinted glass. Some are assembled as butterflies with at least one butterfly cut from thin ski goggles. The edges of the plate glass panels were ground smooth and holes were drilled in the corners to accept strands of piano wire that hang from screweyes fixed into the top of the window frame. The various lenses offer new views of the garden and in winter cast prisms of sunlight on the opposite wall of the room.

It is so nice to discover a bit of sentimentality in a garden. This Old Town piece seen on Chicago's near North Side starts with a cast iron urn planted with the same kinds of plants, begonias, geraniums and trailing ivy, that were used in our great-grandmothers' gardens. The urn stands, chest-high, in the center of a small front courtyard and gives a hint of a rebuilt and extended pedestal. There seems to be an extra unit plus an expanded base made with a Coca Cola bottlecap sign and a large square baker's breadpan. All is painted a shimmering white. It really transports the standard garden urn to new heights.

den with surplus stones, brick or adobe. Batter it up a bit and clothe it with vines and mosses.

Stretch your imagination, make departures and care not if you are labeled an eccentric. Personal triumphs can set you up.

A Sew-sew Table

Have the neighborhood welder add a metal frame to the top of a treadled sewing machine base. Then order a sheet of plate glass to fit within the frame. Search out a set of ice cream parlor wire chairs and paint them and the table in a matte black to dramatize the wiry silhouettes. If you can find one, add a holder for a string ball as a table ornament. In case you don't remember, these string holders once stood on grocery store counters for wrapping delicatessen meats and cuts of pound cake.

The bowling ball ornament was pinned to a stout post with a steel rod as the connector. It is one man's memorial to the end of his own bowling career and the mark of his new venture into vegetable gardening. The post is a piece of a utility pole that was discarded by a utility crew.

The eyeglass lenses mounted on plate glass rectangles, again with superglue, suggest another kind of glass salvage. The lenses were accumulated from old family frames and through the

Other Dividends

There are side benefits to this gathering of oddments. It puts you in touch with a shadow world of weird collectors. Some may be scholars of history, some kooks. But life is exciting among the appreciators. On any gloomy day there is the possibility of a rainbow—a rare find, a true jewel. And the days that follow are mellowed while you ponder methods of restoration and installation.

Heart-warming ideas

While we are becoming more aware of energy-saving-techniques to keep our homes warm, we might also check into ways to keep our gardens comfortable enough for use on cool evenings.

One of the best ways to hold the warmth of the sun into the twilight hours is with a stone terrace paving. This may sound prohibitive in cost, but there are opportunities in this area too. Flagstone sidewalks in old neighborhoods are often ripped up and carried away as part of the deal by cement contractors laying new sidewalks. The price is right but the stone is heavy. If it can be broken into smaller fragments as it is removed and trucked directly to the buyer's property, the project is easier, but still no cinch. The terrace space needs to be leveled and prepared with a six-inch layer of sand. The stones are then brought in, one by one with the help of musclemen. The entire paving is set to a slight angle away from the house. This gives the best drainage. Good soil should be set in the crevices, and sedums and other succulents planted within.

The flagstone offered at building centers is

much thinner and easier to install, but it holds less heat. The warmth of a good stone terrace carries over into the fall, and even the winter, melting snows and drying the area faster than in surrounding drifts.

Solar stoves made of reflecting metal can be made by craftsmen from patterns relayed to us from India. These are cooking devices that require no other fuel than the sun.

The columnar kerosene heater shown requires an expensive fuel but it can warm a small area quickly and attractively. Its cast-iron grill holds heat even after the wick is snuffed out.

A man in Los Altos, California, made a barbecue out of a charred whiskey barrel. He sliced through the top about five inches down and added a back hinge, to hold the lid. Then he added a metal grill inside the barrel and 16 inches down to hold the charcoal, and he was ready to set up his alternatives. With a second grill above the charcoal he could grill steaks, with the electric spit he could turn a roast. If he wanted to smoke a piece of meat he could lower the barrel lid and let the process begin. What ash falls through the grill lands on a charred surface and is supposed to remain dormant until it is removed. However, if I were building one of these I would check and double-check for fire danger each step of the way.

A Bowl of Warmth

The hog-butchering kettle was salvaged from a farmyard near Long Grove, Illinois, and put to new use as a free-standing fireplace. It was tilted to one side on a three-inch-wide iron ring and filled halfway with sand. The fire is started with dead twigs and broken branches and then stabilized with regular firewood sufficient for an evening's enjoyment. The heat travels into the iron itself and warms visitors sitting to either side as well as out front.

The mobile fireplace among the pines is a local improvisation. The house has a concrete deck on three sides, and the winds shift unexpectedly. Therefore the gardener added three wheels to his pre-fab fireplace and moves it out of the wind when need be. Firewood is stored under the benches on three sides.

A family in Boulder, Colorado, has a terrace ornament that matches the season. It is a three-foot-wide circular pit, edged with brick and half-filled with sand. In fall and winter when a fire is desirable it is used as a firepit, but in late spring and summer a recirculating fountain attached to a circular plastic dish is set down on the brick rim and wired for action. The splash of the water is modest but pleasant and the firepit is hidden from view. The fountain is also a safety cover, protecting guests from a misstep.

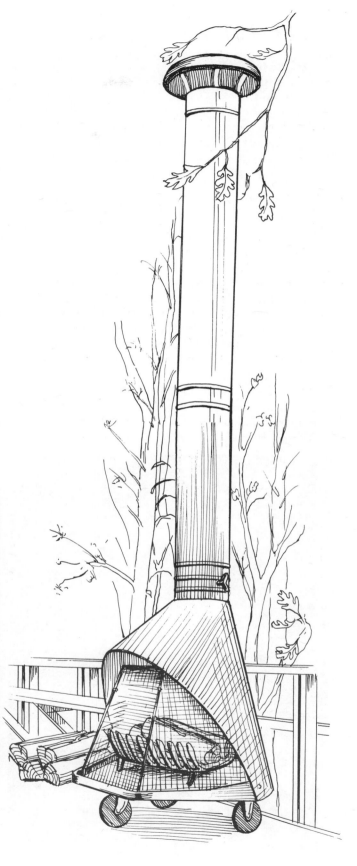

Frightful solutions

It just doesn't pay to make scarecrows that are merely utilitarian. You will never get rave reviews from the crows; in fact they show no appreciation at all. If you are going to indulge yourself in this age-old and seldom successful practice for scaring off predators, you might just as well satisfy yourself and make creatures with a touch of class and a bit of style. Otherwise scarecrowing is no fun at all.

Improvise, as usual, with the things you have at hand. If you are trying to protect your strawberry bed, stuff a pair of nylon stockings or pantyhose with straw and shape a dancing lady. Add a topknot of straw for grace and hang a couple of small mobiles to her arms. Make the mobiles using squares of shiny metal so they will glint in the sun and, hopefully, scare the robins away. The lady will get wet in the rain but with a nylon casing she will also dry out quickly.

As you can see I am stressing the decorative angle because the only way you can have strawberries is to grow enough for both the birds and your family. Actually there is another way. You can grow the fruit within frames that are covered with net. In fact, netting or fruit caging is essential if you are earnest about protecting a crop. In England fruit cages are widely used. Gardeners there go so far as to grow pear trees on a single stalk leaning away from the sun so the fruit ripens equally and can be harvested quickly.

Gardeners have trouble with birds. They enjoy their company but resent the birds' voracious appetites. There is the constant desire to protect them from cats and other hazards but it is never easy. For years birds have been slamming onto plate glass windows to their own discomfort. Some people keep their draperies drawn to lessen the danger. A few enterprising souls have evolved another scheme. They tape a black paper cutout, a silhouette of a large hawk, on the glass to scare the smaller birds away from the glass. Those who use this device say it works fine.

In the community gardens on the outskirts of Minneapolis, scarecrow design is an important art. Each gardener sets up his own hallmark, in part to scare away the birds but also to reveal to their community neighbors a little about themselves. These vegetable plots attract participants from all walks of life. A mother and young son tend their row crops right next to an executive who grows nothing but leaf greens for his gourmet salads. Some gardeners run out to their gardens during their lunch hours to munch on carrots

special coral color and the slacks a bit worn. But the black and white blouse is a real zinger. If it doesn't scare the birds away it should at least give them a migraine. From the looks of the garden around her few crops have grown or else the birds have taken them all away.

But scarecrowing, you may have noticed, is changing in other ways. A large mail order company is offering a wash 'n wear scarecrow of vinyl in bright colors. You pump it up yourself and hang it up on the cross tree. It is very convenient, but then what will you do with your old clothes?

As a final touch another seed company is offering an inflatable snake with a diamond-back look. You just blow it up to its full six feet and place it in your garden, moving it about every few days, to protect against birds and rabbits. The advertiser boasts that it is so realistic it will fool a few people too.

while they harvest other vegetables for the evening meal.

The scarecrow with the golf hat must have been outfitted in the family laundry. He is dressed in a tired T-shirt and old-fashioned jeans. His head is a liquid bleach bottle and his features defined with a felt-tipped pen. He seems a bit indifferent, with his drooping work gloves and his lackadaisical expression. Incidently, the work gloves that hang on these 'crows' are all in good condition. They are used by the gardeners when they come out to weed.

The scarecrow in the Mexican hat couldn't care less. He doesn't even raise his arms to scare the birds away. The patches he wears on his suit coats were added on, indicating a bit of slumming. The jeans seem in good condition although they may be worn out in the seat. The head is a stuffed pillowcase and a little big for itself. The coat has torn since it was hung on the frame and the weather will make it more appropriate in time. Still it is nobody's Ray Bolger and it is apparent that it has never traveled the yellow brick road.

The buxom lady in the polka-dot blouse appears well-corseted. Her figure is maintained by the dressmaker's dummy beneath, and her head is a wig stand. Her scarf is chiffon and her sunglasses quite chic. Her rubber gloves are a

Improvisations for the future

As though to condition us for the nuclear age, a utility company on the West Coast has designed an ornamental garden on a hilltop near San Luis Obispo. The design is embellished with such futuristic oddments as massive steel slabs, huge electrical insulators, super pipes, a torturous collection of valves and an array of reinforcing rods as thick as fence posts. All these ornaments were originally fashioned and machined for the Diablo Canyon project.

Nuclear Samples

The garden designer invites us to see, in a neutral setting, how beautiful these items can be. The garden also suggests how the surpluses that accrue in our century might become the treasured fragments of the next. This presumption of future value sounds valid since many of us today are

using relics from the eighteenth and nineteenth centuries to decorate our twentieth-century gardens.

The grand scale of most of the items displayed seems awesome and the tie-in with a controversial power plant makes some of the visitors uneasy. It is true that the ornaments echo the same sense of drama found in museum sculpture today. They adhere to the principle that 'form follows function'. Shapes are comely and of good color and handsome texture. Still the intent of the products is remembered and makes us leery. It may take time.

Through the years we have learned to place confidence in engineers who dam rivers and build our bridges, in architects who shape great archs and towers and in economists who manipulate and manage our national economy. It may take a while longer for us to place the same confidence in our nuclear scientists.

Enjoy Abstract Forms

In the garden it seems best to focus on abstract forms, the sweep of a curve, whether it is on pipe or leaf, the sheen made by sunlight whether it glides over a steel slab or a flower petal or the thrust of a textured column whether it comes from a stout reinforcing rod or a slender tree.

In this garden we can savor the warmth of the sunlight, the perfection of the circle and the shimmer of a glowing surface and let the rest come. Gardeners have always been escapists and still are.

Three sections of pipe, shown in column one, catch the light of the sky on their inside surfaces, making it bright blue. The reinforced outer casing in rust red becomes a pleasing contrast. Each pipe is about three feet in diameter, indicating the size of the entire assemblage. For those who wish to know more, there is an information display indoors.

Reinforcing rods, and nuts and bolts, are mounted together as abstract forms. The bolts, big enough to sit on, are somewhat disconcerting to the gardener who normally deals with ⅜ inch stock. The fence of wood has an intriguing feature. With one board left out of each panel the visitor feels comfortably enclosed but still has the opportunity to look out at the countryside.

The maze of elbows, pipe joints and valves is

the only piece that suggests a bit of humor. To the layman it appears funny although there is just a chance that it comes 'as is' from a plant installation.

The steel plates, six inches thick, are tied together with cake-sized nuts. The upright element is a section of I-beam with a diagonal cut. The design is more in step with modern art concepts than any of the ornaments. The steel shelf may be intended as a bench but to sit upon it would seem disrespectful and, if the sun was hot, a little warm.

Ornaments for the 21st Century

If I were to choose the fragments of this century that I would use in a garden in the next, it might be a unit in the train that climbs to the top of the Golden Arch in St. Louis, an elevator door from the Chrysler Building in New York or an architectural remnant from Grand Central Station. I might use an 18-inch slice of the cable from the Golden Gate bridge in Frisco or a section of railing from the Glen Canyon dam. I could use a balcony section from New Orleans or a section of their 'corn fence'. If someone offered me a piece of wood from a cherry tree that once grew beside Washington's tidal basin I would shape it to good

use. There is thick colored glass in the Air Force Academy chapel, gargoyles on old churches and a fine lion in a park in Las Vegas, New Mexico, that I favor. But these decisions will be for others to make. I'm sure they will choose more wisely than I would.

It would be good if they loved older things, fences and benches that we admired, trees that we revered and symbols that we honored. I hope also that there will be birds and butterflies and many of the flowers that we presently admire.

Friendly signs

The art of improvising works as well on people as it does on places. If you can put together a gate design that provides protection and also delights your visitors, you have the gift. There are signs and symbols in almost everything we do and these form a language we should understand.

The owl gate reveals exceptional talent in upgrading an ordinary product. A thick paneled door, probably second hand, was embellished with a wood carving of a strange family of owls. The carvings show skill and wit.

These creatures serve as monitors, looking down on each visitor, as if making inspection. Any guest who gets past them must feel relief and pleasure in their approval. The carving, though primitive in style, shows the mark of a professional. It appears to be embellishment enough for any in-town entry door. The garden court in Chicago is lush and secure behind this locked barrier.

If there is any question about the wit of the door owner it should be confirmed by the hint of whimsy in the collection of strange tiles set in the wall above the door frame.

When it comes to locks and gates, some gardeners make use of the latchstring, which they literally let out when they feel sociable and pull in when they prefer to be alone or when a visitor would be inconvenient. This subtle sign is sometimes lost on people with strong knuckles who are determined to get in.

We have a strong latch on our sun garden gate that opens only from the inside, a space which we have access to through our bedroom. From the outside the gate looks to be a continuation of the tall fence that encloses our sunbathing bench and our clawfeet bathtub. For party events, when privacy is not a concern, the double gate swings open to create one more area where guests might wander.

Ring Out Your Presence

In the middle of Colorado, one man has a ship's bell from his sea-going uncle. The two-foot high silver bell hangs on a stout post beside the garden gate. Guests are expected to ring it (there is a pull rope) before stepping inside. Because the bell looks so strange, so far from the sea, visitors find it a friendly sign and come to expect an easy encounter.

Latched but Friendly

The garden gates at Colonial Williamsburg are most always latched. Those that are *open to the public* are so noted on a small sign on the front of the gate. The visitor needs only to reach over the fence and lift the latch to get in. To me this is a good sign. It indicates that the garden is valued and cared for, and it makes each person's visit within seem more privileged.

Gardeners who live in Carmel, California, are beset by curious tourists. They are often strained, keeping people out without appearing rude. A few of these people have designed gates that serve as an optical barrier to be opened only with a lock and key. But the gesture of friendliness still prevails. The gates often include one peekhole, a perforated tile or a latticed panel so that those whose curiosity knows no bounds can catch a glimpse of the 'private' garden.

Welcome Design

The entry bench at right appeared under a time clock in the Found Art chapter. The bench design gives evidence of one gardener's concern for the comfort of his guests. The seat is angled to better fit the form, and to assure the faster drainage of rainfall. The unit cantilevers out from the wall—a device that needs to be planned in advance. This indicates that this detailing was not an afterthought but part of the original plan. The wood is smooth where it needs to be; the velvet-leafed Kalanchoe below as decorative as one would want.

CHAPTER SEVEN

Joyous Color

Be a receptacle. Fill your gardening hours with exciting color combinations and painterly images. Cherish and use all the natural color blends with which the plant world is endowed, but then feel free to create a few bold or subtle combinations of your own.

Give sway to your emotional responses to color and to the pleasures that vivid or pastel hues might provoke for you. While you are building up your courage for new departures, rely on old standby harmonies. Start with a mix of rosy and golden hues but then, on occasion, inject some brighter carnival colors. Do a test run with bold reds, raw purples, or insistent oranges, and mix them in one or more ways to discover all their florid combinations.

Let Nature Reign

Study with pleasure the quiet ways to use blue-on-blue in a shaded place and take note of the incidental surprises a shaft of golden sunlight might add. Let Nature reign, but stand at her side. Be ready to point out the joys that are evident in accidental color and in all other happenstances.

Exercise your own personal taste in color, even if your friends find it a bit odd. Have confidence in your own creations; they are sure to be better for you than would imitations of someone else's choices. Use your talents and your taste with sureness and flair. Sometimes even Nature falters. If so, step in and lend her a hand.

If only as an exercise, try dissonant color. It is a tool favored by many artists before you. Combine clashing hues for the sheer excitement they can engender. Juxtapose brilliant orange marigold beside scarlet salvia and magenta flowering kale. Use lavender *Veronica* and purple *Rudbeckia* in front of a stand of raw yellow *Achillea*. Track down some green zinnias, so popular a few years ago, and put them in the near company of red and pink *Dianthus* and bronze rocket snaps.

If you are uncomfortable with these bold strokes, turn to more subtle variations. Combine delicate 'Spring Song' hybrid columbines with perennial lemon lilies, *Hemerocallis flava*, or plant crystal pink tulips, between stands of rose-colored bleeding hearts, *Dicentra spectabilis*.

A Span of Colors

Take notice of the color variations that develop between a new and a faded bloom. The colors of one climbing rose may span the spectrum, changing from burnished orange to faded pink and be beautiful in each stage of flowering. Recognize these color shifts where you find them. Exploit these plant phenomena when they can add to your palette, but try to use a few miracles of your own.

Use light wisely. It plays a vital role in any color display. Lilac-blue iris are most resplendent when viewed in the cool light of a morning overcast. When they stand in the bright sun, color losses occur. They seem to fade to a dull white, regaining their beauty only after the afternoon shadows lengthen. Knowing this, plant iris where they get enough morning light to dry dewdrops off their petals before they magnify and stain the blooms, and enough midday shade to prevent the fading. Iris appear most dramatic spotlighted by the last ribbons of sunlight from the afternoon sun.

Depend upon brilliant annuals for good midday displays. Red and purple petunias somehow retain their vigor in spite of the heat of the high-noon sun. Grow lavender and white *Dictamnus*, also known as gas-plant, burning bush and dittany, in a central bed for upright growth, but enjoy them more during the early and later hours of the day when their translucent beauty is most evident.

Moonlight Color

Use white flowers by themselves for a moonlit garden or in clumps as a neutralizer between plants of dissonant or saturated colors. By daylight daisies and white phlox go unnoticed beside their more colorful cousins but by moonlight all white flowers stand out as glistening treasures.

Pink *Filipendula* in new bloom is as exquisite as fine lace and this feature is especially evident when the plant is grown near and accented by flowers of stronger colors. For an extra touch add a few brushstrokes of rose *Lythrum* and the violet-hued *Campanula glomerata*.

A garden that is all sun or all shade can be a bore. For a lively distribution of color, plant enough trees to give you a pleasant mingling of each.

Think long on background colors. The neutral tones of concrete walls and terraces, or bleached wood fences are dull but safe. There are other more inventive possibilities. A green embankment of ivy or euonymus can be a useful accompaniment. A distant bed of flowers in a complementary color can make the flowers in the foreground sing. A pool of dark water can add contrast and a touch of mystery.

As you design and choose, think as an artist. Strive for little touches. Gather together a high-key assemblage of feathery flowers in pastel hues, or, if it is more to your taste, the real-life bounce of primary colors.

Find Your Favorites

Try if you can to handle your colors fearlessly—with the spontaneity and confidence of the very young. Find a style and stay with it, at least until you find something better. If it is more to your nature, dash off in all directions exploring all the possibilities. The potentials are almost overwhelming.

But in your own garden, away from the eyes of critics and helpful friends, resist the overwhelming. Instead, treat color as a remarkable tool, a miracle element, and yourself as a catalyst that modifies and increases the wonders color possesses. Devote at least one season to color and its

manipulation as a prime goal and then see if you can ever again ignore it.

Do not take color opportunities lightly. The manipulation of color indoors may be an easy matter today. A spray can of enamel can effect a change in an hour or less. But in a garden it takes longer. It takes time to decide which plants produce the colors you want, to grow those plants and bring them to flower.

And flowers alone are not the whole story. You should also consider the colors of foliage on tree and bush, and the shape of each color mass. To maintain the durability that is desirable, you have to learn what plants need and how you can supply these needs.

We all recognize color as a major garden device, but we use it less than we should. As our temperaments dictate, we can be gentle or daring. We might build up bright reds in front of distant greys to give the illusion of greater garden depth, or reverse the process and the colors if we want to jar our visitor's sense of what is near or far. We can find pleasure in cultivating flowers of a single hue, all pink for an impressive spring display, or icy blue to penetrate cold morning fogs. If we are unable to use our gardens except in the twilight hours, we should plant great sweeps of white phlox, *Cleome*, Shasta daisies and feverfew to shimmer in the disappearing light, and to tempt us to linger longer with the moon. Is any other garden element more obliging?

Brilliance

Brilliance is a word with at least two meanings. It deals with vivid and glorious color and with keen intelligence. The photograph below, made in Carmel, California, gives evidence of both kinds of brilliance. The gardener, having no true garden to work in, used his front steps for a lavish display of nasturiums and lobelias. To these he added an accent of golden yellow pansies, *Viola tricolor hortensis*, as grace notes and a scattering of Lady Washington geraniums, *Pelargonium domesticum*. His keen mind can be recognized and acknowledged easily, but the brilliance of the flowers will need to be visualized because of the limitations of a black-and-white print.

Visualization is a trick worth learning. Bring to mind the yellows and oranges of nasturiums with their bright-green circular leaves. Remember the strength of the blues in lobelia flowers, and imagine how they must look together. The pansies will have a neutralizing effect and the pink geraniums will interact with both the nasturiums and the lobelias.

Complete the environment with white walls, rose-colored brick and grey stone. Decide in your mind's eye what color the plant boxes must be, dark grey or forest-green. If you can master this kind of visualization, the translation of your own garden from a plan to reality will not come as a color surprise.

I am asking you to visualize the garden below first, because I do not have a color transparency of this particular subject and also so that you will realize how much the beauty of a garden depends on color.

Refer to Color Plates

Because the color plates appear in this book's separate color sections I am hoping you will refer to them often while we comment on theories of color that we consider important. Some of the color plates show gardens reproduced elsewhere in the book in black and white. You may find it good practice to visualize color for these black-and-whites based on additional information gleaned from the color plates.

Make it Brilliant

The golden *Calendula* and greyed Dusty Miller, *Senecio cineraria,* shown in Color Plate 9 gains its sense of brilliance from the addition of the vivid magenta blooms of the ice plant, *Mesembryanthemum crystalinum*, and from the flowing distribution of colors. As a test, lay your fingers over the purple hues and notice how much impact is lost. This is not to suggest that you add magenta to every plant grouping, but that you have it in mind when you wish to call attention to a particular area of the garden.

Magenta and purple are fine colors for adding zing to the 'zeenery', but they should be used in small doses or you will have impact in every corner of the garden, and drama nowhere.

Color Plate 12 of a *Bougainvillea* vine, suggests the vigor and vividness of this handsome ornamental, but the excitement of this particular planting is heightened by the vine's close association with the stained-glass window installed in the partition wall. The plant contributes to the structure and the structure to the plant.

A reverse view of the stained-glass window is shown in Color Plate 3. Here in a garden entry room where the light is softer, the colors of the glass are complemented by the rich green tones of the giant Australian fern. Colors, like those in rainbows, should not have to stand separately. The blue morning glory welcomes the company of vining green; the cerise bougainvillea, in this case Barbara Karst, benefits from the blues and purples in the glass.

In Color Plate 26 of an entry door, the shaded greens of the trees are sparked by clusters of pink hydrangeas in the foreground and these two colors in turn are bounced about further by the touch of bright blue in the umbrella stand by the front door.

The lavender crocuses in Color Plate 21 ac-quire an added translucence from the dark browns and greys of the rocky setting. Their fragile quality points up the hazards of spring.

Your Color Sense Matters

Your personality has a strong influence on the development of your color garden. If you are the orderly and cautious type you may test color by planting only a few choice strains, perhaps a few pastel shades of Pacific Giant *Delphiniums*, some pink or white Oriental poppies, *Papaver Orientalis,* and one or two plants of the vivid blue alkanet, *Anchusa azurea*, in the first year. If you are enthusiastic and energetic you may plant every kind of color you can purchase or obtain as a gift, and try them all at once.

Neither extreme is ideal, but to each his own. There should be an approach somewhere in between for all of us. Admittedly there are distinct advantages to being orderly, in not having to redo later, but there is also excitement and delight in learning a lot fast, plunging into the complexities, and becoming acquainted with many varieties quickly. There are sure to be discards and new favorites, the approach can be hectic but the results rewarding. In short, underplanting is barely acceptable and overplanting is a common fault. Interplanting may be a good compromise. Here you test an idea in small spaces, on the bare ground between existing plants. If you already have a fine stand of golden day lilies, plant a few *Anchusa azurea* in vivid blue behind the lilies. Add a few *Rudbeckia* among the *Achillea* to push the goldenness of flowers further, or some pink chrysanthemums to grow among the *Physostegia*, the blue or white compass plant.

If you are displeased with the bedraggled look of ripening tulips, interplant with *Trollius* in golden yellow or feverfew, *Chrysanthemum Partheium*, in daisy-white, but with very bright green foliage.

If you want a trial run on bright vining colors, plant Scarlet Runner, *Phaseolus coccineus,* or Scarlet O'Hara morning glories, *Ipomoea,* to run up strings on a back porch. If later you don't like them, you can pull them out easily.

Each hour of the day has its own rewards, the early unfolding of a cluster of blue flax that fade by midday, *Linum grandiflorum,* the high-noon stability of cerise and purple zinnias, and in the evening the pale translucence of columbine. Each is a minor miracle awaiting your notice.

Fig. 16. Purple crocus announce the coming of spring under a mountain privet, while last year's plants lend color to a strawberry jar. *(Pages 161 and 162)*

Fig. 17. Caryopteris or blue mist shrubs hold seed pods through winter as dried bouquets. They need pruning in spring for blue summer flowers. *(Page 162)*

Fig. 18. Fine stonework shapes a curving retaining wall on a hillside site. Straw cushions and a choice of sun hats make guests feel welcome. *(Page 18)*

Fig. 19. Flowering kale in purple-red and chartreuse makes a dramatic planting when teamed with great mounds of giant lemon-yellow marigolds. *(Page 163)*

Fig. 20. A bottle tree is an old tradition in the South. This departure, using colored glass, captures sunlight and holds it brightly. *(Page 116)*

Fig. 21. The pale lavender species crocus marks the end of winter and the beginning of spring. The rock and curled wood magnify its delicacy. (Pages 160 and 161)

Fig. 22. A streetside view of the skylit cubicle shows a wrought-iron furnace grill on the wall and a box of succulents on a tree-stump pedestal. *(Page 64)*

Fig. 23. A bronze peahen by Edgar Britton struts among the trollius and tulips in the spring. Later, as plants grow higher, she is moved to the lawn. *(Pages 114 and 136)*

Fig. 24. This Grecian antique, half-woman, half-monster, finds new company among potted geraniums and petunias. *(Page 109)*

Fig. 25. Trimmed each year after flowering, these apple trees assume topiary forms and offer a flowery greeting in an entry garden. *(Pages 50 and 166)*

Fig. 26. Potted hydrangeas offer seasonal accent beside an entry door. The Chinese glazed vase holds walking sticks. The bell announces guests. *(Pages 50 and 160)*

Fig. 27. Two tree wells built around venerable live oaks form a retaining wall for a hilltop location, and add seating space as well. *(Pages 18 and 50)*

Fig. 28. The light that comes through the white cloth of this awning made from artist Christo's Running Fence is luminous and flattering—great for party events. *(Page 37)*

Lavender, naturally

If you are about to design a new spring garden or redo an old one, plan first for a coordinated color scheme. If the thought of color control worries you, relax. Spring flowers are the easiest of all to handle. With few exceptions they are just naturally harmonious.

Start, like the song, with lavender-blue dilly-dilly, lavender-green, and make these your major colors. Lean toward blue or pink, as you wish, and add a few splashes of golden yellow to accent and complement. Choosing lavender as a color base, you suddenly have scores of early blooming bulbs and perennials to work with. It becomes clearly evident that in spring Mother Nature is partial to mauve and magenta—in fact that she favors all the purple hues.

Fine Spring Project

Doing and redoing a garden on the basis of color can be an invigorating project. It gives you an excuse to dig up and give away all the vivid red and bright orange plants in your garden, any and everything that clashes with your new scheme. Find a new home for those tall red tulips, the prolific scarlet poppies and the orange iris you bought as a novelty.

Then give focus to the lavender-blue Virginia bluebells, *Mertensia*, that are already doing well under the oak trees. Cultivate a wider spread of violets, and in white and rose too. Carve a rambling path toward the wild blue columbine so you might more often watch them dance their way through spring in pirouettes.

Order some of the self-color all-blue or all-purple pansies as seedlings, and plant them near the kitchen door to greet casual visitors. Lift and separate overgrown clumps of creeping phlox, particularly those in lavender and magenta shades. Replant them where they might creep over a walkway or hang from a garden wall.

Plant Flowering Shrubs

As spring progresses plant new stands of English and Persian lilacs near a fenceline eventually to create a fine spring backdrop. Then add a few forsythia in a sunny, protected corner where they will grow and bloom yellow-bright.

Do an inventory of your early lavender and blue perennials. If you don't have them already,

add creeping Veronica, *V. officinalis* or *V. repens*; the pale blue lace flower, *Scabiosa*; the sturdy blue-flowering ground cover, *Ajuga reptans;* catnip, *Nepeta cataria* or *N. mussini;* and periwinkle, *Vinca minor*. Search out some early-blooming China and alpine asters, *Callistephus*, and painted daisies, *Pyrethrum* or *Chrysanthemum coccineus*. Acquire, from a friend, a clump of *Campanula glomerata*, a hardy, double-flowering bellflower that forms brilliant blue clusters. Divide the clump into at least six parts and start a new bed apart from all others. It is invasive but handsome to those who appreciate robust growth.

Lavender-Flowering Bulbs

In the fall, add a bushel of bulbs having flowers with a lavender cast. Buy the bulbs of squills with tiny blue flowers, *Scilla sibirica*, grape hyacinth, *Muscari,* for its blue to purple grape-like spikes, and crocus in all its lavender variations. See them in Color Plates 16 and 21.

All this done, you can wait for spring with high hopes, knowing that the show will be harmonious. Leave nothing to chance. Nature takes care of the things you may have forgotten. Her apple trees will blossom in pale pink, the pears in white, peaches in a bright rose-pink and cherries in feathery clouds of white.

Continue into Summer

Actually there is no reason why this spring harmony can't drift along through the poppy, peony and rose seasons. There will be no friction if you stay with the pastel shades. Oriental poppies are available now in pink, white or mauve; Iceland poppies in white, peach and golden yellow. With peonies you should pass up the reds and maroons and focus on great whites with yellow stamens, single or double pinks and a lavender or mauve hybrid.

With roses, control is somewhat more difficult. Forego the scarlet, coral and blaze hues and select from fine pinks, whites, a few lavenders or pale and cream yellows.

If you turn to annuals for summer bloom, use restraint. Choose from lemon yellow marigolds, pink and white zinnias, lavender, pink and white petunias to protect your color scheme. As annuals peak, the taller summer perennials compete for attention. Magenta *Lythrum* and *Liatris* grow tall and slender. Nodding goldenrod, *Solidago, Achillea* and blue and white delphinium add taller spires. The purple coneflower, *Echinacea angustifolia*, comes into bloom along with the golden hybrid chrysanthemums, the latter carrying over golden hues well into fall.

Then seek out Japanese anemone, *A. japonica*, a late-flowering perennial of great charm. Its flowering stalks produce single flowers from September to frost, in pink or white.

The Lavender Alternative

If, after a year of concentration on lavender and golden hues, you feel denied the more vibrant colors, take a sabbatical next year and do the clashing thing. Your garden is yours to shape and color. All I am suggesting is the lavender alternative.

Color Me Lavender

The large lavender hybrid crocuses in Color Plate 16 are today's favorite harbingers of spring. While the strawberry plants stand withered and rust-colored in the jar, the crocus introduces a new season with new colors. The crocus bulbs are protected through the winter by the white-barked privet, *Ligustrum,* and sheltered by its branches from late spring snows. The terra cotta hue of the strawberry jar acts as an odd-color complement to the lavender flowers.

The small sculpture in the *Iris* Color Plate 10 exists in a lavender world. The iris are miniature tall-bearded in blue and white, and the sweet rocket, *Hesperis*, dapples the scene with lavender florets and sweet fragrance. The figurine of the thin lady in the big hat is by Meg Anderson of Parrot, Georgia.

With the help of grey-green, lavender-blue carries nicely into summer. In Color Plate 8, a large Russian olive tree, *Elaeagnus angustifolia*, dominates an entry garden. The walkway is edged in blue lobelia and the front door is painted a matching color. The winter view of the Blue Mist shrub, *Caryopteris,* as shown in Color Plate 17,

reveals one more advantage of this 'lavender' plant. A robust shrub with a minty scent, it comes to bloom in August and September with showy lavender-blue blooms that remain on the stem in the fall and dry to a charming bouquet for winter enjoyment. This blue 'spirea' grows rapidly and needs to be trimmed drastically in the spring to maintain control. The plant has two disadvantages: It is self-seeding, so much so that you can supply all the relatives, and the blooms are so laden with nectar that the bees hover over them for weeks. Just don't plant it near a swimming pool!

Dissonant Hues

Some of us have a barbaric, almost vulgar, love of color. Our gardens spill over with shocking pinks, iridescent purples, electric oranges and the wildest of the magentas. At our direction they mingle in the most smashing combinations.

A generation or so ago such blatant color was scorned, but now, with the advent of Day-Glo printing inks, fluorescent T-shirts and paintings where colors come together as in a cymbal clash, dissonance has become an acceptable art form, and a garden opportunity.

In recent months I have been intrigued by a bulb garden filled with dozens of cerise and orange tulips planted around a terrace equipped with standard wrought-iron furniture. But the cushions on the chairs and lounges were of a singing magenta or purple. The dissonance was discord enough to make me shiver with excitement.

These excursions into wild color are standard trips for the professional artists who may spend a lifetime looking for their right colors; such trips can also be a season's entertainment for the gardener looking for new color experiences.

Strong Colors, Sharp Contrasts

If this kind of shenanigan intrigues you, join the club. The opportunities are almost endless. Color Plate 19, of flowering kale and giant marigolds, exhibits the excitement I am trying to describe in words. The forms are different and the colors sharp. Strong sunlight heightens the contrast further.

The hybridizers and seedsmen understand the potential, and labor each year to widen our choices. We have already reached the point where day lilies are available, not only in golden yellow, but in purple, red, brown, peach and melon. Iris are now offered in black, orange, amethyst, rust-red and numerous iridescent shades. The traditional pink peony is being superceded by raspberry cream, dark maroon, or yellow and white with gold tufted centers.

Choices Wide and Wild

All these temptations make our lives more complicated. We are beset by the confusion of wide choices. For some this is difficult. Like interior decorators, most of us do our best work with a limited palette or budget restrictions. To cope with this ever-broadening spectrum, we need to try each segment separately or ignore the opportunities and stay with run-of-the-mill pinks or blues.

Good Blues Rare

If we are to study all the new introductions offered and particularly those receiving All-America Selections designations, we should have the privilege of making suggestions. The hybridizers, it seems, have hit a snag in their search for true blues. Blue ageratums are most nearly lavender, blue iris have the color of faded jeans. Even blue flax veers toward lilac. Only blue lobelia and blue gentian deliver the colors they promise.

Novelty is often the buzz word. We have frilled and ruffled, plicatated and bicolored iris, single, double and picoteed begonias, butterfly and rocketed snapdragons, and Oriental poppies in at least ten colors, with and without blotches.

If you are a beginning gardener, take heart. Veteran plantsmen are forever playing catch-up. One way to escape the confusion is to ignore all the new temptations and concentrate on old favorites. But that has dangers too. You might miss out on something sensational that could lead you off on a new tangent that would occupy you for months, and take you willingly into the realm of dissonant color.

Hybridizers are actually admitting that they have gone as far as they can go with marigolds, zinnias, petunias and snapdragons, the big four, and are now concentrating on lesser flowers, impatiens, celosia and ageratum.

It is enough to make an indecisive gardener weep. But there is some help in sight. Suppliers and greenhouse growers have begun making decisions for us. They no longer grow all the varieties for which seed is available, except on prepaid order from particular customers. They restrict their stock to old standbys and the newest and brightest introductions—take it or leave it. How else can the color-confused gardener survive in this world of too many choices?

Impact with Annuals

Annuals are by far the most remarkable, the most varied. They can provide clashing colors if you wish them, pastels if you prefer, and they can do this in three to four months from seed, or two months from seedlings. With them you can fill out your garden in short order, and with flowers that will continue to bloom all summer long. You must choose varieties that like your climate, sun or shade, moist atmosphere or dry, and give the plants continued care.

Decide what you want most, overflowing bloom, wild color, vining plants for quick shade, tall plants to hide eyesores, fragrance, evening beauty or cut flowers for indoor bouquets. Use the big four where you can and then try other annuals for special use. For bright and vivid hues try *Salvia* with spires in red, lavender and purple, *Celosia* or cockscomb in plumed or crested reds and gold, *Gaillardia*, daisy-like in red and bronze, asters in all pastels, and *Amaranthus* as a crimson fountain of flowers and red foliage.

For fragrance try *Nicotiana*, nasturium and *Verbena*, for foliage color *Coleus* and flowering kale.

For unique form use pansies in single colors with pretty faces; foxgloves, *Digitalis*, a biennial with nodding spires; the Lace Flower, *Scabiosa* in blue and white; Velvet Flower, *Salpiglossis* in bold colors—July to frost; *Cosmos* which thrive on neglect, with hundreds of flowers on fern-like stems; cornflower, *Centaurea*, known too as bachelor buttons and sweet sultan; *Calendula* or pot marigold which thrives until frost; and hollyhocks, *Althaea*, which bloom the first year from seed.

As edgings there are sweet alyssum, lobelia, candytuft, impatiens, portulaca, ageratum and California poppy. For climbing you might try morning glory, moon vine, Thunbergia, *Cobaea scandens* and Japanese hop.

Start annuals from seed in starter trays near a bright window, or from purchased seedlings in May and set outside directly. These are the colors available to you quickly. You choose the colors you want for your palette. Make them mild, make them wild, the opportunities are yours to grasp.

Lively Combinations

The garden shown in Color Plate 14 is both flamboyant and dissonant. The tumbling display of color creates a playful mood, annuals, perennials and roses mix in harmonies and discords, but always with vigor.

The playfulness is also evident in the petunia tree on the terrace in the middle distance. Pink cascade petunias are potted up and stood on a triple shelf within a sphere-like form mounted on a three-inch steel post which in turn is 'planted' in a weighted Versailles topiary box. As the season progresses the petunias cascade over the clay pots, hiding the framework and making the petunias look like one large ball of flowers. The effect is startling, particularly when the colors chosen are cerise or purple.

Joyous color that sings of spring

It is all a matter of focus, of bringing your talents together on a single season. Any time of the year you can add plants and features that will further the idea of what spring should look like in your garden.

Garden miracles do not happen overnight. They take thoughtful planning and execution, starting now if you hope to have an elegant display by next spring. This is based on the assumption that you already have a start on a garden with a few shade trees, some sturdy evergreens and an encirclement of good shrubbery.

Use Flowering Trees

Search out and plant good container-grown stock from your local nursery. Select several flowering trees as spring ornamentals. Choose from apples, pears, cherries, peaches and apricots, according to the tolerance of your climate. Include several crab apple trees for spring bloom and the chance of fruit in the fall. The crab has become a national favorite because of its availability in many hybrids, for as many climate zones.

If you live in an area that is mild and moist, you might also include dogwood, *Cornus*, in one of its varied forms; magnolia, *M. soulangeana*, and wisteria, a beautiful woody vine.

To assure success first choose plants that have been known to flourish in your kind of soil and climate conditions. Then, if you wish to be daring, try a few rare specimens. Just remember that dealing with unknowns is always a gamble.

Among spring-flowering shrubs are the forsythia; flowering almond, *Prunus glandulosa, P. nana* and *P. triloba; Viburnum Burkwoodii* and *V. Carlesii;* bridalwreath, *Spiraea prunifolia, S. Vanhouttei* and *S. Bumalda Froebelii,* and honeysuckle, *Lonicera.* In milder climates use azaleas, camellias, gardenias, jasmine, *Jasminum* and rhododendrons in evergreen and deciduous forms. Plant these shrubs where they will stand out in bloom against dark-green shrubs or tree-shaded areas.

Arrange your plant material to produce surprising vistas as you wander through the garden. Design some fine window views for your enjoyment when rainy days keep you indoors.

Stay with small, healthy stock that roots in quickly. Young saplings are less expensive and easier to plant. They catch up with their larger counterparts in short order.

With the woody stock in the ground, concentrate on herbacious plantings. Add *Trollius, Pulmoniaria, Mertensia, Doronicum,* golden alyssum, and bleeding heart, *Dicentra spectabilis.* For fun and zest add sweet woodruff. *Asperula odorata* and strawberry, *Fragaria.*

With all these plants installed and growing well, get ready for the fall planting of spring-flowering bulbs. Plan for at least a basketful of these little miracles. Include crocus in both its delicate species and hybrid forms, grape hyacinth, *Muscari;* snowdrops, *Galanthus;* and *Scilla.* Tuck them in groups in small places in the shelter of overhanging shrubbery or among colorful rocks.

Add a selection of species tulips, *Tulipa Kaufmanniana, Gregii, Dasytemon,* and *Praestans* for their early, ground-hugging beauty, plus hyacinths, narcissi and golden daffodils (a narcissus) for bolder but still pastel accents. Use the species tulips in rock plantings or beside a walk where you can enjoy a close view and more of the fragrance. The narcissi and daffodils do best in a naturalized woodland setting where they may increase in number without encroaching on other plants. On arid land try the Pasque flower, *Anemone Pulsatilla,* for early blue flowers; in mild, moist country grow the poppy anemone, *A coronaria.* The first is fragile in appearance, the second bold and beautiful. In northern states plant the poppy anemones in the spring.

Make room for several kinds of giant hybrid tulips. They offer a tremendous show in late spring. Choose yellows and whites in cupped and lily forms. Enjoy their vigor and their perfect blooms.

Think twice before adding red, purple and maroon varieties. They are more difficult to see and they tend to call attention to themselves rather than contribute to the total spring scene. It is better to plan on drifts of one color tulips than to get caught with bargain package assortments in two or three colors. The cost is higher but the quality is better and the display more unified than a random color scheme.

Then, before you store your spade for the winter, persevere a while longer. Remembering where the bulbs are planted, scatter the seeds of Iceland poppies and pansies in the spaces between. If you have sweet violets in back corners of the garden, gather them together for a new planting around the bulbs. Or plant strawberries over a new drift of daffodils. You can then enjoy a fruit crop while the tulip blades are ripening. Remember to leave the leaf blades to ripen in place. They bring nourishment to the bulbs for the following year.

Finally, plant primroses beside your garden path, either this fall or early next spring, as your climate will allow. To increase the spring fluff add candytuft, *Iberis* and snow-in-summer, *Cerastium.*

The winter that follows may pass more slowly while you wait for your garden to unfold in its new glory. Get all your other work done early so when spring finally does arrive you will have time to enjoy it.

It Takes Time

If the results fall short of your expectations, be patient. New ornamental trees and shrubs mature more slowly. The second spring should be better than the first and each year thereafter more beautiful than the last.

The spring garden shown in Color Plate 7 has a sense of celebration. It has spring bulbs, daffodils, tulips, and the tuberose, *Polianthes tuberosa,* with waxy-white flowers. It should be planted out in the spring from offsets of the tubers. Flowering almond shrubs in white parallel the wall of the house, and a red-veined crab apple stands at mid-ground. Its blossoms are a richer pink than most crabs.

The globe-shaped apple tree in bloom in Color Plate 25 is in the entry court of the same garden. It is pruned each year after blooming, to maintain the more precise form.

A narrow spectrum

Too many people, when they become involved in gardening, attempt to grow every plant and flower their climate will allow, and this they do in as many colors as the hybridizers can provide.

However, there is a band of gardeners whose numbers appear to be growing who claim a wiser view. They believe that 'less is more' and the better garden is the simpler garden. By design and choice they grow fewer plants and to a narrower spectrum.

This theory may seem startling but it is not much different from the views of 'architects of gardens' as voiced at the turn of the century. They espoused the theory that only two elements were needed for the perfect garden, simplicity and breath of treatment. Simplicity to them meant harmony, and breadth was their way of defining unity. They admitted that there was a third essential, variety, but concluded that this was not in the province of the gardener. They believed that Nature alone would provide variety enough.

Today more and more people are coming to the conclusion that color becomes more difficult to manage as the palette is broadened. Misused or overused, it can create confusion and unrest. Just as interior decorators make color charts for the approval of their clients, so too can a gardener learn of color pitfalls. A hypergreen lawn surrounded by trees and shrubs in strange colors and flowers in hues that are unfamiliar can look as uncomfortable as such colors would seem on a color chart.

There is pleasure enough in medium greens. It is better to err toward dullness than toward conspicuous intrusion. Old English gardeners thought of green as Nature's livery. They would have frowned on the practice of adding too many stripes and bright buttons to the uniform green.

Narrow spectrum gardeners who concentrate on green suggest we avoid the novelties—they live too long. And curiosities do not automatically mean charm. Normal plants are not distressing, strange hybrids can be.

For those who think of their gardens as a stage on which to express their color preferences, there are many design opportunities. Because color carries a message of its own beyond its brilliance, certain colors convey particular qualities that can set the mood of a place.

A golden garden might be planted in an open section with nothing but yellow flowers glowing in the bright light. A shady corner could include some blues or lavenders for gentle contrast. An all-pink or rose-colored garden with azaleas and rhododendrons is claimed to be the most sensational in the spring. But don't make the mistake of thinking that if pink is good, red would be better. An all-red garden would be too jarring for continued use. And avoid designs using color complements. Blue with orange, yellow with purple, or red flowers on their own green stems can result in a volatile scene. Don't strike too loud a note, you may spoil your garden song. Citing the British again, they like to use many varieties but generally only one hue.

Garden movements of this kind start small with a few ardent individuals. Gradually the theories they champion catch on. We now hear frequently of Twilight Gardens, for the work-a-day gardener, All-white Gardens to enjoy by moonlight and Spring Gardens for those whose allegiance is divided between gardening and summer traveling. Others design Secret Gardens hidden from public view and Tapestry Gardens where perennials and shrubbery are so mingled and touching, one plant to another, that the garden seems to be a tapestry of color. Some believe that a garden should begin and end with evergreens. Through every season they provide a point of reference with their cleanly silhouetted forms. They do not change with the season like their deciduous neighbors, from profuse stands of foliage to bare-bones skeletons. The framework and scaffolding of conifers are always apparent.

In deciduous gardens the green-on-green blending of summer is broken before it gets tiresome by the individuality of plants in fall. Oaks change first to bright-red and then rust, poplars, green ash and aspen from cadmium yellow to dirty brown. Suddenly each tree is standing apart for the grand finale. Fall coloring we accept as festival costume for normal plants, but shrubs that are strangely colored year around are looked on less cordially. We should make a rule to allow no more than one or two curiosities in our garden schemes or we will destroy the tranquility we claim to crave.

If you are allergic to sun or if your days are crowded with other obligations, take advantage of the twilight hours. In summer a softness settles over the land as the sun goes down and light-colored flowers acquire a strange luminosity.

Fragrances are more pronounced and privacy, edged by darkness, seems real. To follow this bent, increase your collection of white and pastel flowers. For late spring use daisies, iris, peonies and day lilies. Follow these in summer with spidery *Cleome, Santolina, Dictamnus, Phlox,* Shastas and *Rudbeckia.* As summer mellows, make use of chrysanthemums, Michaelmas daisies (a perennial aster), goldenrod, *Solidago,* Godetia, and cosmos. For fragrance use evening primrose, *Oenothera,* and *Nicotiana.*

Throughout the summer rely on roses for evening shimmer and fragrance. For the safety of your guests keep your paths smooth and your lawn free of obstacles. If you entertain in your garden arrange your parties for the full of the moon, and then add candlelight when it becomes too dark to see otherwise.

In shaping all-green, all-gold, or all-white gardens we have no desire to upset conventional gardeners, but rather to simply titillate ourselves.

However, we should not abuse this garden freedom by creating things that are simply bizarre or eccentric. Our lives are already fragmented by messages and images from distant places; it is better that we express ourselves as best we can in simple ways. Poet Robert Browning once wrote, "If you gain naught but simple beauty, you have gained about all there is."

Color comes with as many names as there are flowers: buttercup-yellow, rose-pink, and poppy-red. But what with the work of hybridizers, poppy-red is no longer description enough. Oriental poppies now win attention with such names as Tangerine, Salmon Glow, Bonfire and Harvest Moon. Coral bells, *Heuchera sanguinea,* is now more than sanguine; its colors include rose, pink and white.

In brilliance, zinnias exceed all other flowers, from standard red and candy stripe to yellow zenith, purple giant, firecracker, lipstick, torch and plum. For years I have been fascinated by the names for colors that people dream up, ecru (light tan), puce (purplish brown) and café au lait. I have yet to encounter a fashion color called French Nude, though I can guess its hue. I am puzzled by another Parisian color named Wild Pigeon. I cannot guess its pigment, unless it is chalky white.

Luis Barragán, an architect of international reputation, claims that "color is functional. It can make a house peaceful, joyous or erotic." He did not say whether these same principles might apply to gardens. However he does believe that an artist should work to one end of the spectrum or the other.

The Zen garden shown in Color Plate 2 reveals the beauty of a green-on-green garden. While the shifts in color are subtle, there is a degree of contrast in the greys of the stone and the blue of the sky. With color limitations there is time to enjoy the thrust of the scrub oak and the convolutions of the land. Bright flower colors that interrupt and capture attention are missing but have not been missed.

The color plate of cacti in grey-green (13) demonstrates the impact that occurs when unity of color allows the eye time to dwell on form and texture. The other plant grouping of burnished orange succulents standing in terra cotta pots in the hot sun, Color Plate 15, is doubly intriguing because the color shifts toward green or brown are slight. As long as we have golden sun and blue skies we can all think well of color, and garden pleasures will survive with bold and subtle colors.

CHAPTER EIGHT

Sensations

One day soon sit down in your garden and become aware of your body. Close your eyes and listen to your own breathing. Feel the weariness give way in your head, your arms and your legs, right down to your toes. Let your mind ravel out until it thinks of nothing. Listen for a while to the sound of the wind. Become aware of one particular scent; let it be subtle, not overpowering. Touch the warmth of the sun on your arm.

Open your eyes just long enough to discover a single color and then close them again on the memory. Look again for a color that excites and a third time for a hue that seems to offer peace.

In the shade of one of your trees sip a glass of tea with a spot of honey or taste the handful of strawberries you gathered just moments before. These become the special moments when gardening is most valued and the world seems far away.

Actually, to survive we must lose our minds and come to our senses. We must learn to use our eyes and ears, our tongues, noses, and fingers to feel and perceive. We need to lean down close to the earth to sense the rhythms of growth and the vibrations of beauty. Each of our trees becomes a friend and each blooming a reunion.

Feel the Sun, See the Flowers

With a garden we do not need mountains or seashore. We need only to feel the sun we see, view the flowers we grew, and watch the stars shine overhead at night. These are the small things that make us content.

Of course to create a garden we must do practical things about soil and drainage and cultivation, but the sensuous approach is equally important in making a garden work. Take time to languish, on occasion, under the trees you have grown, beside the flowering shrubs you have tended. Sit easily and enjoy the place you have formed. Have a quiet ceremony for one to commemorate all the effort that has gone before, the digging and doing, the staking and stooping. Admit it was worthwhile. Let the world go by as you sit in your green-gold place, protected from the elements— noise, dust and people. Some days are especially good. Your senses are better refined, your heart is tuned. Start the day making value judgments. A fresh eye is a stimulant. Plan and plant for a natural flow of line. Staccato accents are hardly conducive to relaxation.

Find 'Positive Wellness'

With vital senses and an intrigued mind you can forget worries and embrace life. Gardening is, in addition to all else, a way of keeping yourself well, a condition known among zealous health addicts as 'positive wellness'.

Each of us is a sensitive energy system that must flow freely to work properly. The vigorous exercise we get in our gardens will help to unlock bodily tension and allow us to respond emotionally.

As we use and develop our five senses we are supposed to develop a sixth sense, not based on the other five, that gives the mind power to know what happens outside itself.

If there is to be joy and comfort in a garden, there must be people to sense it. We know we need places to wander, benches to sit upon, lounges for sunbathing, shaded corners where we can read, and tables where we can dine together. Just the combination of sunlight and open air is sufficient to make it a human habitat, but the addition of a dining porch that has most of the comforts of an indoor room can be a sense-able

idea. If the area is sheltered from the weather by day and warmed by a fire in the evening our senses will be further pleased.

Sniff the Scent of a Shower

For an evening party, after a witheringly hot day, I like to hose down the trees above, the plants beside and the dining terrace around to give the relief and the scent of an afternoon shower. One woman, I'm told, goes further. She swings a fly swatter gently among her scented geraniums on one side and her mint and tarragon on the other to intensify the garden's fragrances.

The sense of smell with many of us is not sensible. The odor of marigold, allium and achillea is too strong for some, and craved by others. The lily of the valley is indeed pleasant, but it is also an opiate. My mother once soothed a small, but controversial, board meeting by locating a huge cluster of these lilies in a cut glass vase in the center of a table. Before the evening ended the members had mellowed, and they departed as friends.

Dance, Meditate or Chant

Each day can be a heady experience. If you are so inclined you can dance in the rain, meditate in the moonlight, do your oms in bright sunlight or chant at midnight. These things and much else await your considerations.

If it is in your nature you can run amok in the Lilac Tide. The lilac does not tell you that spring is coming, it is an emblem that spring is here. Lilac week is a time of tender green and amethyst, and with the hum of bees the very voice of spring.

To us, each gift in its time. The crocus would not be impressive among the summer flowers but it is a thing of beauty as spring moves in.

If tulips send you, know that you are not alone. The famed herbalist Parkinson said centuries ago:

"Tulipase do carry so stately and delightful a form and do abide so long in their bravery, that there is no Lady or Gentleman of any worth that is not caught with this delight."

Taste Unexpected Privileges

Some of us care more about the doing than what is finally done. We become acquainted with Nature and experiment in fragmentary ways, sensing and groping often for greater satisfaction. Others think it vain to dwell so much on oneself, but in our gardens, who can tell? There are so many unexpected privileges. We can learn of new plant materials, study historical viewpoints, or tackle landscape design. We can develop an eye for good sculpture or put together a frivolous assemblage of strange oddments. Our sensitivities have always been there. It is just a matter of switching from familiar to unfamiliar fields of endeavors.

See, Hear, Smell, Taste and Touch

If the switching seems a difficult process and your first efforts to explore the senses should fail, start again with a transcendental garden. Contrary to normal expectations it need not be mystical or metaphysical. It just needs to rise above your previous efforts, away from the intellectual and toward the sensuous.

If these exercises sound like follies and foibles and a kind of corruption, dwell for a while with the songbirds you hear, the vistas you know and love, the vegetables you grow and eat, and the prickly plants you touch. Take note of the many herbs you sniff and taste, and all the other seeing and hearing you take for granted. Count these experiences as the blessings they are and you should be happy in your garden. All these approaches are not so alien, one from the other. Be sensible always.

The sight and sound of water

A water feature to see and hear, no matter how small, can be a wondrous addition to a garden. It need be no more than a series of expanding ripples, a two-step waterfall or simply a smooth reflection, and still serve as a symbol of an elemental force that is essential to our very existence.

To the gardener, H_2O is obliging. It will assume many shapes, it can be playful or serene, sparkling bright or dark and deep; it still retains certain constant attributes. It is willful. It seeks its own level, reflects light and flows easily. In combination, these attributes are the source of its ever-changing beauty.

Spread it out in a quiet pool and it will mirror color and be moved by the wind. Move it from one level to another and it will tumble over lipstones or thread out into crystal-like beads, while adding its own gentle sound of music. Water can be beautiful, even when thrust into the air from a lawn sprinkler or a misting hose, particularly when backlighted by the sun.

We have many choices. We can sculp a very shallow pool, five feet in diameter, seal it with a black, waterproof skin and fill it with three inches of water to mirror a favorite flower bed. When the water evaporates we sweep the puddle clean and refill for further reflection.

We can countersink a shallow tub in a marshy place, surround it with woodland flowers and enjoy it as a watery jewel. We can carve a perfect ten-foot circle no more than six inches deep, mount a bubbler fountain in the exact center and a small recirculating pump beneath, and enjoy the ever-expanding ripples as the changing light falls upon them.

On a more ambitious scale we can bisect a garden with a meandering rivulet to carry water across a natural drainage, or we can cut a narrow and precise canal across a formal garden and step down the water from one knife-edge to another. This we must edge with wood or metal strips and pave with colorful pebbles.

In all such waterworks, shallowness is to be praised, not damned. This reduces the danger for small children who might find the water a temptation. Keep the project simple; restraint is essential. Avoid a complex arrangement of pools and streams in a rock garden. Shun the three-tiered, plastic waterfall that trickles nervously, purring through its motorized cycle.

In a small garden a little pool, rill, or brook is enough. Mirror a garden scene with a bit of color. If there are shade trees overhead, prune so

enough light shines through to make the water sparkle. Select trees that do not shed and produce litter.

That water enlivens and brightens there is no doubt, but its use as a decorative element is still overlooked by many knowledgeable gardeners today. Could this be the year when you will try your skills?

Claude Monet thought of his water lily garden as a work of art. For thirty years he planted it, painted it, and planted some more. There is a hypnotic quality to water movement, an exuberance captured in no other way. It mingles well with yellow flag, *Iris Pseudacorus*, and the marsh marigold, *Caltha palustris*, and with mallow, *Malva,* and meadowsweet, *Spiraea alba* or *latifolia.* Remember too that a dragonfly will skim and hover over a small garden pool as happily as over a lake on a grand estate.

A small frog, like this one from Williamsburg,

can spout fresh water into a pool or be the source of a recirculating fountain, aerating the water along the way. And the flow doesn't need to be decorative. Just the sound of water trickling in a pool or a cave-like place can enliven a garden scene.

There's a fountain at Chatsworth in Derbyshire, England, shaped of copper to look like a willow tree. Fine jets of water spring from the crown of the tree to glisten and fall back into the basin. It may sound modern, but it dates back to the 1690s.

If all else fails design a puddle pool to channel downspout water to where you want it or where it is needed. It helps brighten the day.

A lipstone added to a small stream can make a pretty waterfall and create a new pool above. This natural stream, Cheyenne Creek, collects sun and sparkle as it is now 'allowed' to flow, and makes gentle music.

The scent of flowers

"With life," the saying goes, "it is not how long you make it, but how you make it long." To live without an awareness of the scent of flowers is one way of shortchanging yourself. What could be better, at the end of a day, than to remember the scent of violets or hyacinths, the fragrance of lilacs, daphne in May and June, or the perfume of jasmine or honeysuckle soon after. Such are the pleasures you might have missed had you stayed indoors or hadn't noticed. Knowing and enjoying the scents in a garden can be good sense for all of us. They are among the outward stimuli that nourish and delight our minds.

The sensuous use of space is an art that often develops slowly. As you design you need to visualize how the space will look, how it will feel and what its fragrances might be. You alone can heighten this garden experience. Choose some plants just for their scent, narcissi to welcome spring, sweet violets in May and nicotiana or phlox for summer nights. Include nasturiums for their pungent scent, if you are inclined. Some like it, some don't. Its Latin name, meaning 'nose-twister', suggests the debate is long-standing.

Personal preference will be your best guide. We need to be careful, even wary, in our selections. Some smells are delightfully delicate, others overpowering. Jasmine, honeysuckle, and *Viburnum Carlesii* can be disturbing in large doses. Sweet-smelling petunias, used in quantity, can at first seem pleasant, then cloying and eventually revolting. It is up to you to make the selection and gauge the dosage. There is another rule to apply, a pleasantly-fragrant plant doesn't

also have to look good. It is already doing its own thing.

Use fragrant plants beside a garden path where their perfume will be stirred by passersby. Use them carefully, much as a woman applies perfume—a touch on her wrists, behind her ears and in the bend of the elbow, where the pulse stirs most.

Try for lilies-of-the-valley in a shaded corner, a mock orange shrub near the garden gate or peonies, in a great cluster, in the brightest sun. Grow linden, apple, or *Magnolia stellata* for seasonal sniffing, but nose-test black locust, wild plum and certain pears before you give them garden room.

Enjoy iris, day lilies and roses late spring into summer, hardy carnations and lilies, pinks and heliotrope. From among the quick-growing annuals choose sweet alyssum, mignonette, verbena, petunias, four-o'clocks, and sweet sultan.

If you favor their pungent odors, grow marigolds and calendula. Titilate your nose with the fragrant leaves of lemon verbena, thyme, lavender, rosemary, sweet marjoram, summer savory and basil, or the pungent leaves of achillea, feverfew and camomile. Even the scent of chrysanthemum leaves can be a boon while you are waiting for the flowers to bloom. The fragrance is much the same. There are those who favor the smell of the leaves of a tomato plant most of all. They find excuse to stake, tie and stir their plants to encourage pollination, yes, but also to stir up the scent they most enjoy.

Joys for Children

If you have been a slow learner on flowers and scents, pass on the pleasures to your children or grandchildren as you discover them. Play guessing games with the fragrances. Hold dandelions under their chins to see if they like butter. Remove the outer petals from a larkspur floret and show them the tiny rabbit head within. Teach them to make a snapdragon snap, and point out the hearts in a bleeding heart plant. Help them to make dancing dolls from hollyhocks and ballerinas from columbines. Show them how to whistle between their thumbs, using a blade of grass as a reed. Braid a white clover chain long enough and stout enough to make a crown. Send them packets of flower seed with their birthday cards. Take them on a seed-gathering walk in early fall, and help them plant the seeds they have gathered. Bring them a bouquet of fragrant flowers when they graduate, from kindergarten, grade school, high school or college. The gifts you bring from your garden can be the most treasured of all.

There is an ebb and flow to gardening, a surge of bloom followed by a quiet retreat. When bloom is full, fragrances are many, when the ebbing occurs, we rest too, preparing ourselves for the next gifts of fragrance.

Iris and Day Lily

Double your pleasure and your fragrance potential by choosing plants known to smell good. Do a nose-garden focused on flowers with agreeable odors. Train sweet-scented vines over gateways and doorways or around an ornament at the end of a path. Grow deep blue Siberian iris with buttercups on the shady side of your garden while tall-bearded iris, roses and peonies blossom in the full sun. Grow some of the sweet ones: sweet alyssum, sweet peas, and sweet scabious.

The day lily in the photograph is delicately scented, other varieties are in varying degrees. This flower, Prairie Moonlight, is a chartreuse introduction by a Kansas City hybridizer. Its botanical name, *Hemerocallis*, is from the Greek and means 'beautiful for a day'. The funnel or bell-shaped flowers are clusters on scapes that rise well above the foliage. They open separately, one each day until the cluster is spent.

The sense of touch

On a dreary day go into your garden for solace. Reach out and find something good to touch—the roughened bark of a tree, the smoothness of a warm stone. Sense the unity that exists between a gardener and the land, of live beings growing and evolving together.

We all understand the pleasures in touching our families and our friends, but we neglect tactile opportunities in our gardens. We think too little of the textures of a plant grouping or of the structural surfaces we expect to live with. We accept, heaven forbid, crushed rock in five-ton lots to cover a barren place, without considering fully our alternatives. For a slightly higher investment we might instead have river-smoothed stones, or slices of wood rounds that could lend distinction for years to come.

We need to go sensuous as we water our plants on a hot, summer day. We need to soak up the sun and actually feel the breezes. We can let a little of the water splash on ourselves and feel younger.

Most gardeners have the childish instinct to muck around in the mud, to push things around and shape sand castles. From our gardening we learn body movements to serve through a lifetime. The strenuous activity makes us feel, and feel fully alive. With a chore to do, the mind and the body are focused on a single goal. Our age doesn't matter; in our gardens we thrive, and relish the strength of our muscles.

Georgia O'Keefe, distinguished painter, recalls her first memories as ''something seen with my eye and touched with my hand''. This touching seems very important. We feel good or we feel bad, but we seldom *feel* things with our hands, or our bodies.

Tub Be, or Not Tub Be

The ritual of sun or tub bathing was enjoyed by the Elizabethans four centuries ago. Devotees stripped down in a small 'undressing house', walked across the turf and down stone steps into a pool, to soak or splash in the sun. The ground was carpeted with turf filled with tiny flowers and the space walled with tall hedges. Caged birds sang in niches cut in the hedging. The entire setup was for the full use of the senses, the touch of sunlight, the smell of flowers, the sound of birds, the taste of clean air and the sight of a private patch of blue sky.

Outdoor tubbing today, like many ideas, reached California first. Tubs of cedar or redwood are now being set down in any private garden setting. They are an answer for gardeners who don't want the expense or responsibility of larger pools. Young parents favor them as a way to keep their youngsters clean through the hectic summer months. Rules on skinny-dipping should be set by the gardener alone. For instant nostalgia, set your tub under a willow tree and pretend you are a kid again down by the old swimming hole. This can be a nice dream on a pleasant day, so enjoy it.

The cast-iron tub shown in Color Plate 5 is mostly whimsy. Purchased at an ABC Sale (attic, basement and cellar), it was garnished with sunflowers and set in the sun. It has no water connections, relying on the sun-warmed garden hose for fulfillment. When the plug is pulled, the water drains out onto the fence vines with no ill effects.

Textures Widely Different

To demonstrate the extremes in plant textures, I show the soft, low-growing succulent, *Echeveria*. The rosette-forms make a fine carpet cover on poor soil. These, in Carmel Valley, are displayed in the company of several rock crystals, evident at lower left. The hard, smooth crystals make a fine foil for the soft slightly-hairy plants. This, to me, is the kind of artistry a gardener can practice, exercises that add to one's tactile pleasures.

The prickly teasel is almost architectonic. The rigid design of each bloom is impressive, especially when its spiny edges are backlighted by the sun. Plant it in a corner where it will not spread too far. Both you and the butterflies should be pleased with its presence.

The bristly cacti shown as a group in Color Plate 13 have their own strong textures, both forbidding and tempting. There is something in our nature that makes us want to touch not only the soft and smooth things but also fierce and threatening objects. How many times have you seen a person cup his hand over the needles of a cactus to see how close he could get before he was injured. It may be apocryphal, but I've heard that some cacti needles can sense the warmth of a human passing by and with this information leap out at their victims. That, if true, seems to be carrying the sensitive touch too far.

Sensations for the birds

Songbirds are really co-owners of our gardens. It is our own responsibility to give them food, water and shelter, things essential to their continued occupancy. This we should understand, since the same things are vital to us.

Good bird food is not just a sack of seed from the supermarket, but rather the seeds and fruits of our trees, shrubs and vines. The fruit of Russian olive pleases the robin as well as the squirrel. Apples and pears attract, perhaps unduly, the magpies, starlings and grackles. Finch and juncos seem content with millet and an occasional sunflower seed. Chickadees earn their keep for their consumption of insects, but, given a chance, they are ravenous for sunflower seed. The red cedar, *Juniper virginiana*, is favored by many of our songsters for its blue-black, bloomy fruit.

Robins are partial to holly and firethorn, *Pyracantha*, berries, particularly when the ground is so hard they can't find worms.

Further, if you don't have the berries they want, the birds, wittingly or no, will import their favorite seed and leave it in your garden as droppings encased in fertilizer. The seeds they consume elsewhere go through their digestive tracts unharmed, for reuse. *Cotoneaster, Viburnum lantana, Lonicera,* and mulberry, *Morus rubra,* have all arrived in our garden this way and grown as volunteer seedlings. The mulberry is also favored in farmyards by chickens, hogs and children.

Hawthorne trees are a remarkable food source for our little birds. They retain their fruit into February and March when other supplies are

The *Amelanchier* tree or shrub, known as the shadbush, Juneberry or serviceberry, has fruit like a miniature apple that is bony inside. This is another bird favorite.

The mulberry, mentioned earlier, is the perfect tree as far as birds are concerned, but for many gardeners it is a big headache. The red fruit is messy, staining walkways and lawns. The best solution, if you wish to cater to the birds, is to plant one or two trees in a back corner where their mess won't matter.

Both the wild and the cultivated varieties of chokeberry, *Prunus virginiana*, provide good food, and their blossom and colorful fruit can please you as well. The honeysuckle is worthy of cultivation in most of its 180 or more species, although it is cussed by some for rank growth. Its flowers are sweet-scented and its fruit white, yellow, orange, red, blue or black. In late summer robins scramble over the branches reaching for the tiny, translucent jewels.

The berries you produce are temptations and treats for the birds, who are basically insectivorous. We also need to plant barberry thickets or spiny hedges as cover against their predators. With food, shelter and water, the bird population in your garden can be doubled and tripled. Water is essential for drink and for bathing to keep their feathers in prime condition. Preening with natural oils gives feathers warmth against a severe winter. Locate the birdbath in the sun, above ground and near plant cover. Wet birds are vulnerable to cats.

The partnership between birds and people must be strong because the highest densities occur in home gardens, not wild places. The beauty, movement and song these creatures bring to our gardens is so wonderful that anything we can do to cater to their wishes is but a small courtesy extended to good partners.

Listen in your garden for a bird about to sing.

Fill a window box in winter with the twigs of bittersweet, rose hips, northern holly and add the fruit spikes of sumac.

scarce. *Cotoneaster, Viburnum* and most of the dogwoods, *Cornus*, are excellent food but they are so favored that they do not stay long on the bough.

In winter the raisin-like fruit of the high-bush cranberry, *Viburnum trilobum,* is a true enticement. Cedar waxwings keep watch and arrange their visits just as the fruit falls to the ground for easier eating. The Virginia creeper, *Parthenocissus quinquefolia*, is a favorite for its black fruit. (This is not to be confused with poison ivy.) The *Cotoneaster horizontalis,* its branches laden with bright red fruit, is a delicacy for the mourning dove. Most birds appear to eat the fruit of crab apple trees very eagerly, but I'm told by experts that the birds are really working their way down to the tasty seeds at the heart of the fruit.

Food to savor

"Life," according to Carl Sandburg, "is like an onion. You peel it off, layer by layer, and sometimes you weep." With vegetable gardening it can be much the same. On a big plot there could be day-to-day victories, one upon another, but then the sky can fall in, followed by hail, and you too would weep.

Still, if we live without savoring the taste of good, homegrown vegetables and fine herbs we will be missing too much. We just need fortitude or ingenuity to survive the ups and downs, and the eccentricities of our climates.

In Colorado it takes skill to grow good tomatoes. Local experts set their seedlings in rich, well-watered loam in early spring, surround them with a double stack of concrete blocks and cover all with tough plastic until June 1. Then as plants reach over the rim they are tied to newly-implanted corner stakes. With continued watering and tying, the plants become respectable and produce fruit early and late.

For the fun of it, other gardeners plant bushy tomato seedlings in a plastic bag of rich compost. They set the bag on the terrace, in the sun, slit it

open, set in three or four seedlings and keep the bag moist. This is a fine way to watch day-to-day growth.

If you are looking for another way to grow potatoes, set seed potatoes in a barrel or big box half-filled with rich garden loam. Water them through the summer, adding six-inch layers of soil as the plants grow upward. When the topmost layer of potatoes is mature, dump over the container and harvest your crop. Save the soil if you choose to try the method again another year.

Plant zucchini in a pocket of rich soil on a rise of ground. Enjoy their decorative spread and pretty bloom. Add dwarf marigolds to grow between. Cross-fertilize the zucchini flowers with a soft artist's brush for a bigger crop. Harvest should start in eight weeks.

Set out a circle of carrot seed in a vacant spot in your taller flower beds. Enjoy the fern-like foliage summer into fall. When frosts come, cover the plants with straw, ready for selective harvesting —right up until Christmas. If you miss a few they may come up the following year as tall Queen Anne's lace, the wild carrot.

Grow giant sunflowers along a fenceline for high screening and as food for you and the birds. Beat the U.S. record for sunflower height— seventeen feet.

Edge a sidewalk with salad makings. Try endive, lettuce and New Zealand spinach. Grow fence crops of pole beans, sugarsnap peas, squash or cantaloupe.

Plant a six-foot ring of chives and fill it with pie segments of basil, marjoram, parsley and thyme. Use dill, caraway or tarragon as a center accent.

Plant out asparagus wide and deep in rich soil and rhubarb too, along a sunny boundary line for spring harvest year after year. Add Jerusalem or Chinese artichokes in a back corner for summer flowers and fall harvest of the tubers. Boil and butter them or serve cold with a tangy mayonaise.

Try Spartan Sleeper onion for long keeping, the Earlidew melon, the Square Tomato for paste, and the straight-necked Ingot squash.

For a little off-color activity grow yellow beets, blue potatoes, white tomatoes, Gourmet Globe or Gold Rush zucchini, the latter with yellow meat. There is purple cauliflower and red okra and egg-sized eggplant in white. Yellow Baby is a yellow watermelon and Golden Midget is pink with a yellow rind.

If heat is a problem, try Royal Oak lettuce. If your season is short, look for Early Prolific pepper. If space is limited look for the tomato with large fruit on short vines, Floramerica.

To handle your surplus root crops, sink a barrel in your garden as a root cellar. Fill it with newspaper-wrapped packages of carrots, rutabaga and turnips. Drop the lid and insulate with leaves and a tarpaulin, so you can draw on this supply through the winter as needed.

Grow vegetables that are decorative and useful. Try the perennial multiplier onion with its crop above ground. Plant cabbages, lettuce and chard in a moss-filled hanging basket for orna-ment and eventual consumption. Plant vegetables and herbs in a paved garden with a latticed screen and its own lady bountiful statue. Plant your crops in separate squares of soil countersunk in the brick paving.

If the land behind your house rises sharply, make it split-level with a sheltered lawn beside the house and a level piece of ground above, behind a concrete block retaining wall. The vegetables will get plenty of sun and first dibs on the hillside runoff.

Thoreau of Walden Pond claimed that tending his garden "attached him to the earth, and from it he drew strength."

Butterflies to enjoy

Rabindranath Tagore, the Hindu poet, wrote, "The butterfly counts not months but moments and has time enough." These were words I learned in school and hope always to remember. From these winged creatures we can learn grace and beauty.

The Aztecs believed that souls returned to earth as butterflies and hummingbirds. Some gardeners today share that belief. They even claim to have experienced the presence of an old friend, hovering near.

If for these or any other reasons you would like to add this element of movement to your garden, consider ways to entice butterflies. The idea is not new but it has languished. It takes time, study and considerable patience.

The whole complex process has fascinated ear-lier gardeners, including master statesman Winston Churchill. He noticed the lack one day and immediately set aside a portion of his Chartwell garden for this fluttering breed. The process was not easy. Bringing nests of caterpillars from Europe, he tried to introduce the Black-veined Whites, but the chrysalids were as attractive to English birds as they had been in a previous era, and the genus died out. His attempt to introduce Swallowtails faltered also when his gardener unwittingly cut down a bed of fennel that had been planted as a breeding place and future caterpillar food. He still found joy converting a summerhouse into an emerging-cage where he could sit and watch the chrysalids unfold.

Attracting butterflies with flowers rich in nectar

is easy, getting them to stay is more involved. They favor the honeyed scent of lavender flowers, especially the butterfly bush, Buddleia. In early spring they find the sweet alyssum, wallflower, violet and scabiousa rich in nectar. Among annuals the French and African marigold, candytuft and ageratum are preferred. In midsummer phlox, Sweet William, cineraria, pink sedum, mums and aster serve well.

Butterflies need certain plants for breeding and will lay their eggs nowhere else. Except for the Cabbage Whites, who also like nasturtiums and salad greens, they do little garden harm.

Nettles are tasteful to the Vanessa butterflies; willows and poplar to the Tortoiseshells; Painted Ladies prefer thistles. Peacocks, Admirals and Commas also favor nettles.

For breeding you need a patch of stinging weeds or a clump of thistles. If your garden includes an open meadow of grasses and wildflowers, you can attract, with sorrel, the American Coppers; and with tender leaves the Blues, Ochre Ringlets, Grass Nymphs, and Pearl Crescents will stay nearby, fluttering from flower to flower. The Crescents will lay their eggs in asters. Keep the grasses tall through the end of summer or the caterpillars will die for lack of food. If mowing and tidiness is a concern, skip the whole business.

The Fritillaries, Regals, Dianes and Great Spangled butterflies like sunny woodlands, primroses and violets. They feed at night and hide much of the day. Their caterpillars prefer decaying leaves, so they do little damage.

The Swallowtails are among the most exciting, with thirty species in the United States.

The Papaw butterfly favors the papaw tree, *Carica Papaya*. The Pacific Tiger, a coastal variety, feeds on alder, *Alnus,* and willows, *Salix.* The Spicebush Swallowtail prefers sassafras and spicewood, *Lindera Benzoin.*

To distinguish butterflies from moths, notice the clubbed, thread-like antenna on the butterfly and the feathered antenna on the moth. Butterflies fly by day, most moths by night. Butterflies rest with wings vertical, moths with wings spread.

The life cycle of the butterfly runs from egg to larva to pupa to chrysalid and finally to winged creature. Eggs for a new cycle are laid near acceptable food. The presence of live butterflies in a garden can be far more rewarding than any showcase collection might be. No one, especially a butterfly, would like being pinned down.

As an extra treat, create your own mud puddle club, as a place where butterflies might congregate and drink together. As the sponsor you can be an interested observer.

The butterfly's wings are both lifters and propellers. The aerodynamics varies among species. Monarchs have small bodies and large wings and function more like gliders. Others fly swiftly for short distances. Some migrate, others hibernate as caterpillars or butterflies.

Spiders lay in wait. Birds, frogs and lizards eat them and flies lay eggs on the caterpillars to be consumed by future larvae. Life is not easy.

Pleasures that endure

"If you want to be happy all your life," said famed seedsman David Burpee, "become a gardener." This I consider good advice and I hope that you, my reader, will so agree.

In our garden place we can nourish our love of home, and free ourselves from the instinct for change. There are enough changes in a garden each morning to satisfy our hearts and minds. The more we become involved in our plots, the more we care. And, selfishly, we care more for the plants we have nurtured ourselves than for the finest tree or flower with which we have had no personal connection.

Security and Nourishment

Our gardens offer security, a place at home free from the workings of others, a source of sensual pleasures and, with a small orchard and a vegetable plot, a place to grow good food and save money. Eating our vegetables raw we can gain more vitamins and save energy with less cooking. Then, with enough calcium in our diets, we can keep our bones strong so we can live long and productive lives.

Even the chores of gardening are good for us because strenuous physical activity is good. A garden is almost insurance that we will lead long lives, rich with pleasures.

With our growing desire to be self-sufficient and immune to outside forces, our gardens are an immediate answer, an ever-present refuge. There

we are never lonely, living with the sibilant sounds of birds and insects. Only when a storm approaches and the land is hushed do we miss this friendly sound. The Japanese favor the sound of crickets and of bamboo blowing in the wind. They have been known to select plants for the noises they make.

Finding sounds that please does not always come easily. If we can screen out the noise of power mowers and traffic we can enjoy the songs of birds, the tinkling of bells, and, if we are lucky, the sound of water splashing in a small pool.

Touching and Smelling

Touching also becomes important. We reach for pleasant things to touch, the needles of a white fir, the feathery stalks of rose yarrow. We touch and we smell. We bend to the scent of individual roses, a pungent tomato plant, or we reach to capture and sniff a strand of sweet-smelling clematis.

I can recall no gardener who wasn't happy with his or her lot. I remember meeting a woman, living alone and tending a fog-bound seacoast garden. She was at work in the morning in overshoes and rubber gloves. The garden was lush and overgrown, but glorious, swagged with cerise bougainvillea and hung along the eaves of the house with great pendulous tuberous begonias. Her involvement was a delight to behold.

A retired doctor I know staked his plot on the foothills below Pikes Peak. The ground was rocky and barren but he made it bloom. He negotiated with the people at the rodeo stadium and took away sullied straw and manure by the truckload to dress his garden. He grows his tomatoes in sun pits and his Iceland poppies between slabs of rip-rap. He caters to the bees with a stack of hives and grows beautiful vegetables on his trucked-in ground. His enthusiasm is contagious. I have never seen a happier man.

New Challenges

On a mesa of gravel that reaches down from Ute Pass an energetic woman has taken up challenge gardening. She has had her garden enclosed with adobe walls to shelter it from the persistent winds and frequent thunderstorms, and within that space she has cultivated a garden geared to her

was damaged in both the Revolutionary and Civil Wars. Through ten generations in one family it has reached its present and very enthusiastic owner. Azaleas and magnolias surround pools of dark water that reflect the huge oaks festooned with Spanish moss. When I see him he tells me of the carload of daffodils he added, or his efforts to extend the blooming season through summer. I would rate his enthusiasms as great and almost equal to that of the gardener bent on developing a half-acre plot.

Year-round Involvement

Best of all, gardening is a year-round preoccupation. The plantsman takes pride in his great stone pine, *Pinus cembra*, as it reaches toward the clouds, and the artist/sculptor spends a winter shaping his own metal armillary, to be set in place by early spring. Many of us look out at the snows impatiently and then go back to our books and garden catalogs. Others take pride in the bamboo they planted between the rocks, and enjoy it each day as the snows continue.

If you are one of the impatient ones, always eager for the new gardening year, take comfort in Edgar Wilson Nyes's quip that "winter lingered so long in the lap of spring that it occasioned a great deal of talk."

My wish to you is to be happy and healthy. Enjoy your garden. It's greater than you think.

plot's horticultural limits. She concluded that late spring was her best season. Natural moisture was still in the ground, the sun was bright and adjacent wildings would be coming into bloom. Narrowing her focus further, she realized that mornings were the best part of the day. Winds would be calm and the air cool. She concentrated on low-growing plants that flowered in May and June. Rockrose is a favorite, blue flax second. She planted golden alyssum among her rock-strewn beds, species tulips, iris and miniature roses. On the lee side of the house she put down the rhizomes of Siberian iris and the seed of Rocky Mountain columbine. Along the paths she added woolly thyme and pussytoes. Colorado blue spruces divert the winds that the walls miss. She grows sedums, shastas and gaillardias for color in other than the prime season. With her broad view of the Pikes Peak massif and the Rampart Range, some would say she doesn't need a garden, but she says, "I'm proud. With all the limitations, I've accomplished something."

Size Does Not Matter

A man from South Carolina, the heir to a 470-acre plantation garden, is having an equally exciting time. The property dates back to the 1680s and

Resources

The opportunities, resources, and information available to gardeners can be extremely helpful. Nurserymen and suppliers offer us lists of their wares, public and private gardens are open, most often for a fee, for our study and review. Libraries bulge with horticultural information, and garden publications invite our subscriptions. There is far more available than can be recorded here without starting another book. Therefore I list only those items with which I have some personal acquaintance. Some information changes from year to year so double-check by postcard first on addresses on catalogs and publications.

Publications / Magazines

American Horticulturist, 7931 East Blvd Dr., Alexandria, VA 22308
Brooklyn Botanic Handbooks, 1000 Washington Ave, Brooklyn, NY 11225
Flower and Garden Magazine, 4251 Pennsylvania Ave, Kansas City, MO 64111
Garden, N.Y. Botanical Gardens, Bronx, NY 10458
Gardens for All, 180 Flynn Ave, Burlington, VT 05401
Horticulture, Massachusetts Horticultural Society, 300 Massachusetts Ave, Boston, MA 02115
Lawn Care, Scotts, Marysville, OH 43040
Plants Alive, 2603 Third Ave, Seattle, WA 98121

Also general family magazines—*Better Homes and Gardens, House Beautiful, House and Gardens, Southern Living* and *Sunset.*

Mail Order Companies

Abbey Gardens, 176 Toro Canyon Rd., Carpinteria, CA 93013: *cacti and succulents*

Burpee Seeds, Warminster, PA 18991; Clinton, IA 52732; Riverside, CA 92502: *flowers and vegetables*

California Epi Center, P.O. Box 1431, Vista, CA 92083: *epiphyllums*

Comstock, Ferre & Co., 263 Main St., Wethersfield, CA 06109: *flowers and vegetables*

Dow Seeds Hawaii, Ltd., P.O. Box 30144, Honolulu, Hawaii 96820: *flowers, shrubs, exotic seeds*

Farmer Seed & Nursery, Faribault, MN 55021: *flowers and vegetables*

Dean Foster Nurseries, Hartford, MI 49057: *seeds, fruit and ornamental trees*

Guerney's Seeds and Nursery, Yankton, SD 57079: *flowers and vegetables*

Hastings, 434 Marietta St. N.W., Box 4274, Atlanta, GA 30302

Herbst Bros. Seedsmen, 1000 Main St., Brewster, NY 10509: *flowers and vegetables*

Joe Harris Co. Inc., Moreton Farm, Rochester, NY 14624: *flowers and vegetables*

Illini Gardens, P.O. Box 125, Oakford, IL 62673: *perennials, wildflowers, rock plants*

Jackson and Perkins, Medford, OR 97501: *roses, spring bulbs, perennials, seeds*

de Jager Bulbs, Inc., 188 Asbury St., South Hamilton, MA 01982: *bulbs for all seasons*

Johnny's Selected Seeds, Albion, ME 04910:
vegetables and herbs

Earl May Seed and Nursery Co., Shenandoah,
IA 51603: *vegetables, flowers and trees*

Miller Nursery, Inc., Canandaigua, NY 14424:
fruits, nuts and ornamentals

Geo. W. Park Seed Co., P.O. Box 31, Greenwood,
SC 29647: *flowers, vegetables and plants*

Plants of the Southwest, The Railroad Yards,
Santa Fe, NM 87501: *native seeds, trees and
shrubs*

Rice Nurseries, Lyons, NY 14489:
flowers and vegetables

Sheridan Nurseries, 700 Evans Ave., Etobicoke
M9C 1A3 Ontario, Canada: *ornamental trees and
shrubs*

Slocum Water Gardens, 1101 Cypress Gardens
Rd., Winter Haven, FL 33880: *water lilies and
fish*

Stokes Seed, Inc., 737 Main St., Box 548, Buffalo,
NY 14240: *flowers and vegetables*

Stark Bros. Nurseries & Orchards, Louisiana,
MO 63353: *fruit trees and shrubs*

Thompson & Morgan, Seedsmen, 401 Kennedy
Blvd., Somerdale, NJ 08083: *British firm—
flowers and vegetables*

Unwins, P.O. Box 326, Farmingdale, NJ 07727:
British firm—flowers and vegetables

Wayside Gardens Co., Hodges, SC 29695:
hardy plants, bulbs, shrubs

White Flower Farm, Litchfield, CT 06759:
perennials, bulbs

Dave Wilson Nursery, Hughson, CA 95326:
stone fruits

Horticultural Supplies and Tools

Barrington Industries, P.O. Box 133, Barrington,
IL 60010: *garden and greenhouse equipment*

A.M. Leonard, Inc., 6665 Spiker Rd., Piqua,
OH 45356: *horticultural tools and supplies*

Walt Nicke's Garden Talk, Box 667G, Hudson,
NY 12534: *tools and gadgets*

Public Gardens and Arboretums

Eastern States

Arnold Arboretum, Jamaica Plains, MA 02130
—*265 acres, flowering shrubs, dwarf
evergreens*

Old Sturbridge Village, Sturbridge, MA 01566
—*restoration of homes and gardens*

Planting Fields Arboretum, Oyster Bay, Long
Island, NY 11771—*405 acres, rhododendrons,
camellias, orchids, cacti*

Old Westbury Gardens, Old Westbury, Long
Island, NY 11568—*100 acres, flowering shrubs,
new hybrids*

New York Botanic Gardens, Bronx, NY 10458
—*237 acres, restored conservatory, native
garden, conifers*

Brooklyn Botanic Garden, 1000 Washington Ave.,
Brooklyn, NY 11225—*50 acres, specialty
gardens, roses, water lilies, desert plants*

Cloisters, Fort Tryon Park, New York,
NY 10040—*monastery garden of herbs*

Bartram's Gardens, 54th & Elmwood,
Philadelphia, PA 19152—*first botanical garden
in America*

Longwood Gardens, Kennett Square, PA 19348
—*1,000 acres, large trees, tropical and
sub-tropical conservatories*

Bishop's Garden, Washington Cathedral,
Washington, D.C. 20016—*roses, yews,
and very old box*

Dunbarton Oaks, 1703 32nd St. N.W.,
Washington, D.C. 20007 (not open July to
Labor Day)—*roses, herbaceous borders*

U.S. National Arboretum, Washington,
D.C. 20002—*400 acres, magnolias,
camellias, azaleas*

Winterthur Gardens, Winterthur, DE 19735
(open April through October)—*60 acres,
naturalized plantings*

Colonial Williamsburg, Williamsburg, VA 23185
—*100 small gardens with eighteenth-century
plant materials*

Norfolk Botanical Gardens, Air Port Rd., Norfolk, VA 23518—*175 acres, rhododendrons and azaleas, hollies*

Private gardens on tours in Richmond and Fredericksburg area

Mount Vernon Gardens, Mt. Vernon, VA 22121 —*George Washington's home and gardens*

Monticello, Charlottesville, VA 22901 —*Thomas Jefferson's hilltop home and gardens*

University of Virginia Faculty Gardens, Charlottesville, VA 22904—*small gardens on campus*

Tryon Palace, New Bern, NC 28560 —*restored Colonial gardens*

Orton Plantation, Lower Cape Fear, Wilmington, NC 28401—*ancient live oaks, formal gardens*

Biltmore Gardens, Ashville, NC 28803 —*Olmstead plan (site of film Being There)*

Reynolda Gardens, Winston-Salem, NC 27109 —*flowering cherries, magnolias, day lilies, nativeroses*

Sarah Duke Gardens, Duke University, Durham, NC 27706—*50 acres, spring bulbs, magnolias, crab apples*

Brookgreen Gardens, Murrel's Inlet, SC 29576 —*southeastern natives, sculpture garden*

Cypress Gardens, Charleston, SC 29404 (open February, March and April)—*azaleas and camellias*

Magnolia Gardens, Charleston, SC 29407 —*28 acres in spring bloom, magnolias, azaleas, spring bulbs, eighteenth-century plants*

Middleton Place, Charleston, SC 29407 —*1,000-year-old live oak, formal gardens butterfly lakes*

Private gardens on tour in old Charleston, near the bay

Private gardens and riverfront restoration in Savannah, Georgia

Calloway Gardens, Pine Mountain, GA 31822 —*2,500 acres, azaleas, rhododendrons, dogwoods, resort, golf*

Vizcaya-Dade County Gardens and Art Museum, Miami, FL 33129—*10 acres, formal Italian gardens by the sea*

Middle States

Bellingrath Gardens, Theodore, AL 36582 —*800 acres, 65 landscaped, sub-tropical plants*

Mynelle Gardens, Jackson, MS —*old estate restored, spring display*

Hodges Gardens, Box 921, Many LA 71449 —*garden on old quarry, flowering shrubs*

Longue Vue Gardens, 7 Bamboo Rd., New Orleans, LA 70124—*8 acres in town, interlocked gardens, fountain*

Private gardens, French Quarter, old city —*wander at leisure*

Rosedown Plantation, St. Francisville, LA 70775 —*fine old estate, lathed gazebo, fine gardens*

Tennessee Botanical Gardens, Nashville, TN 37205—*54 acres, tulips, redbuds, fragrance garden*

Missouri Botanical Garden, 2315 Tower Grove, St. Louis, MO 63110—*60 acres in city, 2,100 acres at Gray's Summit, Missouri, Japanese garden, Climatron, succulents*

Fort Worth Botanic Garden Center, Fort Worth, TX 76107—*75 acres, roses*

Carlsbad Botanical & Zoological Park, Carlsbad, NM 88220—*600 acres, desert plantings, ramps for handicapped*

Chicago Botanic Gardens, 775 Dundee Rd., Glencoe, IL 60022—*specialty and handicapped gardens, native trees, lagoons*

Cantigny, Wheaton, IL 60187—*former home of Tribune publisher, Robert McCormick. Wood structure for vines, privacy, great lawn, gardens*

Morton Arboretum, Lisle, IL 60532—*1,500 acres given by the salt king—native plants, reading garden*

Beal-Garfield Botanic Garden, Michigan State University, East Lansing, MI 48823 —*8 acres on campus, large katsura tree*

Matthaei Botanical Gardens, University of Michigan, Ann Arbor, MI 48105—*300 acres, wildings, prairie plants, conservatory*

Dawes Arboretum, Newark, Ohio 43055 —*950 acres, flowering crabs, native forest, azaleas*

Denver Botanic Gardens, 9090 York, Denver, CO 80219—*conservatory and gardens in modern designs*

Arizona-Sonora Desert Museum and Gardens, Tuscon, AZ 85703—*native Sonoran plants, cacti, collection, wildlife*

Boyce Thompson Southwestern Arboretum, Superior, AZ 85273—*30 acres southeast of Phoenix, desert plants*

West Coast

Balboa Park, San Diego, CA 92101—*lath house, pools, sculpture garden, zoo plantings*

Quail Gardens, Encinitas, CA 92024 —*succulents, sub-tropicals, arid land*

Rancho Santa Ana Botanic Gardens, Claremont, CA 91711—*native California plants, 83 acres up hillside*

Los Angeles State and County Arboretum, 301 N. Baldwin, Arcadia, CA 91006—*126 acres, southern hemisphere plants, tropicals*

Descanso Gardens, 1418 Descanso Dr., La Canada, CA 91011—*150 acres, teahouse, flowering trees, ferns*

South Coast Botanic Garden, 26701 Rolling Hills Rd., Palos Verdes, CA 90274—*87 acres, Los Angeles County facility, stone fruits, annuals*

Santa Barbara Botanic Gardens, Inc., Mission Canyon Rd., Santa Barbara, CA 93105 —*75 acres in coastal canyon, natives, ceanothus*

Huntington Botanic Gardens, Oxford Rd., San Marino, CA 91108—*125 acres, palms, conifers, Japanese gardens*

Carmel Mission, Carmel, CA 93921 —*early Spanish gardens around mission*

Antonelli Gardens in Santa Cruz, and Vetterle and Rienelt Gardens in Capitola are both fine commercial displays of tuberous begonias

Filoli Gardens, between Woodside and San Mateo, CA—*National Trust garden of great historical interest*

Tea Garden, Golden Gate Park, San Francisco, CA 94122—*near conservatory, excellent Japanese detail*

Strybing Arboretum, 9th Ave. at Lincoln Way, San Francisco, CA 94122—*open park with fine old trees, plants*

Lombard Street, between Hyde and Leavenworth, in San Francisco, is a corkscrew block south of Golden Gate—*landscaped with hydrangeas*

Muir Woods National Monument, Mill Valley, CA 94941—*magnificent grove of redwoods makes a cathedral-like place*

Portland International Rose Test Garden, Washington Park, Portland, OR 97201—*also rhododendrons, camellias*

University of Washington Arboretum, Seattle, WA 98195—*200 acres, coastal plants, Japanese garden*

The gardens and arboretums listed above can serve as excuses for travel junkets, and for ideas on design, ornamental and plant materials that should be applicable to your own garden, but you do not need to travel so far for help and inspiration. Join your regional horticultural society, plant society or garden club for more precise guidance. Use the services of the USDA Agricultural Extension Services, but don't let them make you fear and dread every bug and disease that comes down the pike. Pursue the pleasures of gardening, and leave the worrying to someone else. Nature heals itself.

INDEX